TEACHER'S PET PUBLICATIONS

LITPLAN TEACHER PACK
for
Pygmalion
based on the book by
George Bernard Shaw

Written by
Mary B. Collins

© 1996 Teacher's Pet Publications
All Rights Reserved

This **LitPlan** for George Bernard Shaw's
Pygmalion
has been brought to you by Teacher's Pet Publications, Inc.

Copyright Teacher's Pet Publications 1996

Only the student materials in this unit plan (such as worksheets,
study questions, and tests) may be reproduced multiple times
for use in the purchaser's classroom.

For any additional copyright questions,
contact Teacher's Pet Publications.

www.tpet.com

TABLE OF CONTENTS - *Pygmalion*

Introduction	6
Unit Objectives	8
Reading Assignment Sheet	9
Unit Outline	10
Study Questions (Short Answer)	13
Quiz/Study Questions (Multiple Choice)	20
Pre-reading Vocabulary Worksheets	29
Lesson One (Introductory Lesson)	39
Nonfiction Assignment Sheet	41
Oral Reading Evaluation Form	48
Writing Assignment 1	55
Writing Assignment 2	57
Writing Assignment 3	59
Writing Evaluation Form	60
Vocabulary Review Activities	53
Extra Writing Assignments/Discussion ?s	51
Unit Review Activities	62
Unit Tests	65
Unit Resource Materials	91
Vocabulary Resource Materials	105

A FEW NOTES ABOUT THE AUTHOR
George Bernard Shaw

SHAW, George Bernard (1856-1950). "I have been dinning into the public head that I am an extraordinarily witty, brilliant and clever man. That is now part of the public opinion of England; and no power in heaven or on Earth will ever change it." George Bernard Shaw wrote this about himself in 1898. He was then 42 years old. A tall, thin, red-bearded man, he was already well known in London as a critic of music, art, and drama. He was an influential socialist speaker, and he had written plays that attacked the accepted ideas of his time.

George Bernard Shaw-often referred to by his initials-was born in Dublin, Ireland, on July 26, 1856, to an Irish Protestant family. His father had a small wholesale business but drank heavily and neglected his affairs. Shaw's mother was a cold, humorless woman whose main interest was music. Eventually she and her husband were separated. His mother's interest in music offered her and her son a means of escape from this situation. She became acquainted with a musician named George John Vandaleur Lee, and in association with him she filled her house with other musicians. Shaw heard so much music during this period of his life that he developed a deep appreciation for classical music.

Shaw's formal education did not last long. He was tutored by his uncle, then attended day schools, in which he was "near or at the bottom" of his class. By the age of 15 he had become a clerk in a land agent's office. He was a good worker, but he saw no future for himself in office work. His mother and sister had left his father in Dublin and moved to London, and in 1876 he joined them there.

He spent his days at the British Museum reading room, writing several novels-all failures-and studying. During the evenings he began to attend lectures and debates, and he developed into an effective orator. He joined the Fabian Society in 1884 and became one of its most active members. In 1885 Shaw was given a job as a book reviewer for the Pall Mall Gazette. This was followed by several other jobs as a critic of books, art, or theater for various periodicals.

Shaw's first play, 'Widowers' Houses', was performed in 1892. This was the first of many plays, nearly all successful. His main purpose as a dramatist was to shock people out of conventional, hidebound ways of thinking. His view of his work was reflected in the title of his collection 'Plays: Pleasant and Unpleasant', published in 1898. 'Mrs. Warren's Profession', which was not produced until 1902 because of censorship, was included in this collection. Shaw labeled such plays as unpleasant because "their dramatic power is used to force the spectator to face unpleasant facts."

The play concerns the inability of one of the characters to accept the fact that her mother, Mrs. Warren, gained her fortune through prostitution. Mrs. Warren is the most conventional character in the play, and she defends her life with an attack on the society that rewards vice and oppresses virtue.

Among Shaw's many plays are 'Arms and the Man' (1894), 'Candide' (1897), 'Caesar and Cleopatra' (1901), 'Man and Superman' (1905), 'Major Barbara' (1905), 'Pygmalion' (1913), and 'Saint Joan'

(1923). Shaw also published many essays, including "The Intelligent Woman's Guide to Socialism and Capitalism" (1928).

In 1898 Shaw married Charlotte Payne-Townshend. They had no children, and Mrs. Shaw died in 1943. His correspondence over the years with the actresses Ellen Terry and Mrs. Patrick Campbell was widely publicized. In 1925 he won the Nobel prize for literature. Shaw died in Ayot St. Lawrence, Hertfordshire, on Nov. 2, 1950.

— Courtesy of Compton's Learning Company

INTRODUCTION

This unit has been designed to develop students' reading, writing, thinking, and language skills through exercises and activities related to *Pygmalion* by Bernard Shaw. It includes eighteen lessons, supported by extra resource materials.

The **introductory lesson** introduces students to one main theme of the play through a bulletin board activity. Following the introductory activity, students are given a transition to explain how the activity relates to the book they are about to read. Following the transition, students are given the materials they will be using during the unit.

The **reading assignments** are approximately thirty pages each; some are a little shorter while others are a little longer. Students have approximately 15 minutes of pre-reading work to do prior to each reading assignment. This pre-reading work involves reviewing the study questions for the assignment and doing some vocabulary work for 8 to 10 vocabulary words they will encounter in their reading.

The **study guide questions** are fact-based questions; students can find the answers to these questions right in the text. These questions come in two formats: short answer or multiple choice. The best use of these materials is probably to use the short answer version of the questions as study guides for students (since answers will be more complete), and to use the multiple choice version for occasional quizzes. It might be a good idea to make transparencies of your answer keys for the overhead projector.

The **vocabulary work** is intended to enrich students' vocabularies as well as to aid in the students' understanding of the book. Prior to each reading assignment, students will complete a two-part worksheet for approximately 8 to 10 vocabulary words in the upcoming reading assignment. Part I focuses on students' use of general knowledge and contextual clues by giving the sentence in which the word appears in the text. Students are then to write down what they think the words mean based on the words' usage. Part II nails down the definitions of the words by giving students dictionary definitions of the words and having students match the words to the correct definitions based on the words' contextual usage. Students should then have an understanding of the words when they meet them in the text.

After each reading assignment, students will go back and formulate answers for the study guide questions. Discussion of these questions serves as a **review** of the most important events and ideas presented in the reading assignments.

After students complete reading the work, a lesson is devoted to the **extra discussion questions/writing assignments**. These questions focus on interpretation, critical analysis and personal response, employing a variety of thinking skills and adding to the students' understanding of the play.

Following the discussion there is a **vocabulary review** lesson which pulls together all of the fragmented vocabulary lists for the reading assignments and gives students a review of all of the words they have studied.

There are three **writing assignments** in this unit, each with the purpose of informing, persuading, or having students express personal opinions. The first assignment is to inform: summarize the information they have found while working on their **group project**. The second assignment is to persuade: students persuade Higgins to treat Liza better. The third assignment is to give students a chance to simply express their own opinions: students explain why some manners are important to have and others are not, and how one can decide which ones are most important.

In addition, there is a **nonfiction reading assignment**. Students are required to read a piece of nonfiction related in some way to *Pygmalion*. After reading their nonfiction pieces, students will fill out a worksheet on which they answer questions regarding facts, interpretation, criticism, and personal opinions. During one class period, students make **oral presentations** about the nonfiction pieces they have read. This not only exposes all students to a wealth of information, it also gives students the opportunity to practice **public speaking**.

The **review lesson** pulls together all of the aspects of the unit. The teacher is given four or five choices of activities or games to use which all serve the same basic function of reviewing all of the information presented in the unit.

The **unit test** comes in two formats: short answer or multiple choice. As a convenience, two different tests for each format have been included. There is also an advanced short answer unit test for higher level students.

There are additional **support materials** included with this unit. The **extra activities** section includes suggestions for an in-class library, crossword and word search puzzles related to the play, and extra vocabulary worksheets. There is a list of **bulletin board ideas** which gives the teacher suggestions for bulletin boards to go along with this unit. In addition, there is a list of **extra class activities** the teacher could choose from to enhance the unit or as a substitution for an exercise the teacher might feel is inappropriate for his/her class. **Answer keys** are located directly after the **reproducible student materials** throughout the unit. The student materials may be reproduced for use in the teacher's classroom without infringement of copyrights. No other portion of this unit may be reproduced without the written consent of Teacher's Pet Publications, Inc.

UNIT OBJECTIVES - *Pygmalion*

1. Through reading Bernard Shaw's *Pygmalion*, students will study the many facets of "good manners."

2. Students will demonstrate their understanding of the text on four levels: factual, interpretive, critical, and personal.

3. Students will plan and hold a formal garden party.

4. Students will consider the importance of good manners and the importance of recognizing when "good manners" are taken too far and create unnecessary snobbery.

5. Students will study the relationships among the characters.

6. Students will be given the opportunity to practice reading aloud and silently to improve their skills in each area.

7. Students will answer questions to demonstrate their knowledge and understanding of the main events and characters in *Pygmalion* as they relate to the author's theme development.

8. Students will enrich their vocabularies and improve their understanding of the play through the vocabulary lessons prepared for use in conjunction with the play.

9. The writing assignments in this unit are geared to several purposes:
    a. To have students demonstrate their abilities to inform, to persuade, or to express their own personal ideas
        NOTE: Students will demonstrate ability to write effectively to <u>inform</u> by developing and organizing facts to convey information. Students will demonstrate the ability to write effectively to <u>persuade</u> by selecting and organizing relevant information, establishing an argumentative purpose, and by designing an appropriate strategy for an identified audience. Students will demonstrate the ability to write effectively to <u>express personal ideas</u> by selecting a form and its appropriate elements.
    b. To check the students' reading comprehension
    c. To make students think about the ideas presented by the play
    d. To encourage logical thinking
    e. To provide an opportunity to practice good grammar and improve students' use of the English language.

10. Students will read aloud, report, and participate in large and small group discussions to improve their public speaking and personal interaction skills.

READING ASSIGNMENT SHEET - *Pygmalion*

Date Assigned	Act(s) Assigned	Completion Date
	Act One	
	Acts Two & Three	
	Acts Four & Five	

UNIT OUTLINE - *Pygmalion*

1 Introduction	2 PV Act One Practice Parts	3 Read Act One PV Acts 2 & 3	4 Study ?s Act One Read Acts 2 & 3 PV Acts 4 & 5	5 Study ?s Acts 2 & 3 Read Acts 4 & 5
6 Study ?s Acts 4 & 5 Extra ?s	7 Vocabulary	8 Library/Project	9 Writing Assignment #1	10 Project Planning
11 Film	12 Film	13 Writing Assignment #2	14 Nonfiction Reports	15 Garden Party
16 Writing Assignment #3	17 Review	18 Test		

Key: P = Preview Study Questions V = Prereading Vocabulary Worksheets

STUDY GUIDE QUESTIONS

SHORT ANSWER STUDY GUIDE QUESTIONS - *Pygmalion*

Act One
1. What purpose does the rain shower serve?
2. The note taker is assumed to be of what profession? What actually is his profession?
3. What does the note taker say about a "woman who utters such depressing and disgusting sounds"?
4. The note taker brags about what he could do for the flower girl within three months. What does he claim?
5. Who takes the cab Freddy brings? Why?
6. What do Higgins and Pickering have in common?

Act Two
1. When Higgins recognizes the flower girl, what is his reaction?
2. What does Eliza Doolittle want?
3. Even after he agrees to teach her, what is Higgins' attitude towards Eliza?
4. Describe Mrs. Pearce's role.
5. Eliza determines to leave rather than to be further insulted. How does Higgins persuade her to stay?
6. What is the point of the bath scene?
7. Mrs. Pearce makes some suggestions to Higgins. What are they?
8. Why did Alfred Doolittle come to see Professor Higgins?
9. Doolittle says, "I'm undeserving, and I mean to go on being undeserving." Why does he not want to better himself?
10. Why does Doolittle want only five pounds instead of the ten he is offered?

Act Three
1. Who are Mrs. and Miss Eynsford Hill?
2. Henry says, "We want two or three people. You'll do as well as anybody else." What does the fact that he says that tell us?
3. What does Liza do wrong at Mrs. Higgins' home?
4. What does Clara think of Eliza?
5. Who is Nepommuck?
6. Is Eliza successful at the ambassador's reception?

Act Four
1. Why did Eliza throw Higgins' slippers at him?
2. What is Higgins' advice to Liza when he realizes she is upset (although he cannot understand <u>why</u> she is upset)?
3. Why does Liza wish Higgins had left her where he had found her?
4. Why does Liza tell Freddy, "Don't you call me Miss Doolittle . . . Liza is good enough for me."
5. What was Freddy doing below Eliza's window?

Pygmalion Short Answer Study Questions Continued

Act Five
1. Why is Henry Higgins concerned about Liza's being gone?
2. Why is Alfred Doolittle upset?
3. Higgins says, "She behaved in the most outrageous way. I never gave her the slightest provocation." Is he lying or not?
4. What becomes of Eliza?

ANSWER KEY: SHORT ANSWER STUDY GUIDE QUESTIONS - *Pygmalion*

Act One

1. What purpose does the rain shower serve?
    It gives the main characters a relatively believable circumstance under which to meet.

2. The note taker is assumed to be of what profession? What actually is his profession?
    The others assume he is a police officer of some kind. He is actually a phonetician.

3. What does the note taker say about a "woman who utters such depressing and disgusting sounds"?
    He says she "has no right to be anywhere--no right to live."

4. The note taker brags about what he could do for the flower girl within three months. What does he claim?
    He claims that he could pass her off as a duchess at an ambassador's garden party.

5. Who takes the cab Freddy brings? Why?
    The flower girl takes the cab Freddy brings. The mother and daughter have left for the bus, and the flower girl feels rich because of the money which Professor Higgins gave her.

6. What do Higgins and Pickering have in common?
    They both study speech.

Act Two

1. When Higgins recognizes the flower girl, what is his reaction?
    He says that "she's no use. . . . I'm not going to waste another cylinder on it. Be off with you; I don't want you."

2. What does Eliza Doolittle want?
    She wants to learn how to speak well enough to be able to be hired to work in a flower shop instead of on the street corner.

3. Even after he agrees to teach her, what is Higgins' attitude towards Eliza?
    "She's deliciously low--so horribly dirty. . . . Put her in the dustbin." He treats her as an object--and not a very nice object, either.

4. Describe Mrs. Pearce's role.
   She is the housekeeper for Higgins and tries to be the voice of reason. ("You mustn't talk like that to her." "But what's to become of her? Is she to be paid anything? Do be sensible, sir."

5. Eliza determines to leave rather than to be further insulted. How does Higgins persuade her to stay?
   He offers her chocolates and promises her taxis, gold, and diamonds.

6. What is the point of the bath scene?
   It shows Eliza has ideas of morals and decency even though she is low-class and "vulgar." She has a personal code of right and wrong and is sensitive.

7. Mrs. Pearce makes some suggestions to Higgins. What are they?
   She asks him to curse less, to not sit around in his robe, to not wipe his hands on his clothes, and to try to be a good example for his pupil.

8. Why did Alfred Doolittle come to see Professor Higgins?
   He wanted to get money for himself, to blackmail Higgins in order to get a little money.

9. Doolittle says, "I'm undeserving, and I mean to go on being undeserving." Why does he not want to better himself?
   If he rises in class, he also will rise in responsibility. He wants a free life, free from responsibility and people's expectations.

10. Why does Doolittle want only five pounds instead of the ten he is offered?
    He can waste five pounds without feeling guilty. Ten pounds would require responsibility.

Act Three
1. Who are Mrs. and Miss Eynsford Hill?
   They are the mother and daughter from the rainstorm in Act One.

2. Henry says, "We want two or three people. You'll do as well as anybody else." What does the fact that he says that tell us?
   He is rude to everyone--not just Liza. He thinks only of his work and himself.

3. What does Liza do wrong at Mrs. Higgins' home?
   She speaks perfectly but tells an odd story of her aunt's death using vulgar, though well-pronounced, language.

4. What does Clara think of Eliza?

    Clara is very taken with Eliza. She wants to use Liza's new small-talk and to imitate her.

5. Who is Nepommuck?

    He is a guest at the ambassador's reception, fluent in many languages, and says he is an expert. He claims Eliza is a fraud, that she is really a princess.

6. Is Eliza successful at the ambassador's reception?

    Yes, she is very successful.

Act Four

1. Why did Eliza throw Higgins' slippers at him?

    Higgins and Pickering had just carried on a whole conversation as if she weren't in the room. They were rude and inconsiderate and treated her unfeelingly. In talking about the lessons with her, Higgins said, "The whole thing has been a bore." "The whole thing has been simple purgatory." After ignoring her through the whole conversation, Higgins has the nerve to ask her to turn out the lights as he leaves the room. When he comes back looking for his slippers, she throws them at him in her anger.

2. What is Higgins' advice to Liza when he realizes she is upset (although he cannot understand <u>why</u> she is upset)?

    "It's only imagination. Low spirits and nothing else. Nobody's hurting you. Nothing's wrong. You go to bed like a good girl and sleep it off. Have a little cry and say your prayers: that will make you feel comfortable."

3. Why does Liza wish Higgins had left her where he had found her?

    "[At the corner of Trottenham Court] I sold flowers. I didn't sell myself. Now you've made a lady of me I'm not fit to sell anything else."

4. Why does Liza tell Freddy, "Don't you call me Miss Doolittle . . . Liza is good enough for me."

    She feels like in many ways "Liza" in her old ways was a better person than "Miss Doolittle."

5. What was Freddy doing below Eliza's window?

    He has fallen in love with her and hangs around the outside of the house hoping to get a glimpse of her.

Act Five

1. Why is Henry Higgins concerned about Liza's being gone?

    Her absence has affected him personally. He misses her services; he can't find anything and doesn't know when his appointments are.

2. Why is Alfred Doolittle upset?
    He has unwillingly come into money and now has the responsibilities of being middle class instead of being "undeserving poor."

3. Higgins says, "She behaved in the most outrageous way. I never gave her the slightest provocation." Is he lying or not?
    No; he genuinely believes that he did nothing. Higgins is blind to his own insensitivities.

4. What becomes of Eliza?
    She marries Freddy, stays friends with Pickering, tolerates Higgins, and runs her own flower shop.

MULTIPLE CHOICE STUDY GUIDE/QUIZ QUESTIONS - *Pygmalion*

Act One

1. What purpose does the rain shower serve?
    A. It gives the main characters a relatively believable circumstance under which to meet.
    B. It symbolizes a washing away of old circumstances.
    C. It sets up the conflict of man vs. nature.
    D. It shows that no one can control the weather. All, regardless of social station, are subject to it.

2. The note taker is assumed to be of what profession? What actually is his profession?
    A. He is assumed to be a college professor, but he is really a newspaper reporter.
    B. He is assumed to be a social worker, but he is really a political aide gathering information for a member of the House of Lords.
    C. He is assumed to be a police officer, but he is really a phonetician.
    D. He is assumed to be a clergyman, but he is really an inmate who has escaped from the insane asylum.

3. What does the note taker say about a "woman who utters such depressing and disgusting sounds?"
    A. He says she "needs the help and redemption of the Lord."
    B. He says she "has had a hard, miserable life, and deserves their pity."
    C. He says she "is a symbol of all that is unjust about the current system of government."
    D. He says she "has no right to be anywhere--no right to live."

4. The note taker brags about what he could do for the flower girl within three months. What does he claim?
    A. He claims that he could get her into a good university.
    B. He claims that he could pass her off as a duchess at an ambassador's garden party.
    C. He claims that he could teach her to speak three languages fluently.
    D. He claims he could have her married to a wealthy member of high society.

5. Who takes the cab Freddy brings? Why?
    A. The note taker takes it.
    B. The mother and daughter take it because they don't want to get wet.
    C. The flower girl takes it; she feels rich with the money Professor Higgins gave her.
    D. No one takes it. The rain has stopped, and they have all started walking home.

6. What do Higgins and Pickering have in common?
    A. They both study speech.
    B. They both went to Cambridge University.
    C. They both hate women.
    D. They both belong to the same church.

Pygmalion Multiple Choice Study Guide Page 2

Act Two

7. When Higgins recognizes the flower girl, what is his reaction?
    A. He says he is glad to see her.
    B. He says she is useless, and he tells her to leave.
    C. He says she can stay and clean house for him if she wants to.
    D. He feels kindly and asks his housekeeper to give her food and clothes and a good meal, then to send her home.

8. What does Eliza Doolittle want?
    A. She wants to marry Professor Higgins and get away from her terrible life.
    B. She wants to learn how to speak well enough to be able to work in a flower shop.
    C. She wants to get medical assistance for her lingering cough.
    D. She wants money so she can leave the city and start a new life.

9. Even after Higgins grants her request, what is his attitude towards Eliza?
    A. He treats her as an unfavorable object.
    B. He changes and treats her very well.
    C. He is indifferent towards her.
    D. He treats her like a daughter.

10. Describe Mrs. Pearce's role.
    A. She acts like the mother Eliza never had.
    B. She adds an air of mystery, as the audience is never certain of her relationship with Higgins.
    C. She tries to be the voice of reason.
    D. She is a symbolic reminder of the next class upward from Eliza in English society.

11. Eliza determines to leave rather than to be further insulted. Higgins uses several means to persuade her to stay. Which of these did he *not* offer?
    A. Chocolates
    B. Taxis
    C. Lavish parties
    D. Gold and diamonds

12. What is the point of the bath scene?
    A. It is symbolic of washing away the old life.
    B. It is a sharp contrast with her previous life.
    C. It shows that Eliza has ideas of morals and decency even though she is low class.
    D. It was merely to provide lightness for the audience in an otherwise serious play.

Pygmalion Multiple Choice Study Questions Page 3

13. Mrs. Pearce makes some suggestions to Higgins. Which of these was **not** one of the suggestions?
    A. Curse less.
    B. Don't sit around in his robe.
    C. Don't wipe his hands on his clothes.
    D. Don't smoke.

14. Why did Alfred Doolittle come to see Professor Higgins?
    A. He wanted to ask Higgins to also teach his other two children.
    B. He wanted to blackmail Higgins to get some money for himself.
    C. He wanted to force Higgins to marry her.
    D. He wanted to wish Eliza good luck and bring her her clothes.

15. Doolittle says, "I'm undeserving, and I mean to go on being undeserving." Why does he not want to better himself?
    A. He doesn't want to lose his friends.
    B. His belief in the class system is so firm that he is afraid to become better.
    C. He wants to have a life free from responsibilities and people's expectations.
    D. He doesn't believe he will be able to keep the money, and he doesn't want to get used to having it and then be disappointed.

16. Why does Doolittle want only five pounds instead of the ten he is offered?
    A. He doesn't think Eliza is worth ten pounds.
    B. He thinks if he asks for less now he will be in a better position later to get more.
    C. He doesn't know how to make change for anything over a five pound note.
    D. His wife told him to ask for five, and he always does what she says.

Pygmalion Multiple Choice Study Questions Page 4

Act Three

17. Who are Mrs. and Miss Eynsford Hill?
    A. They are Pickering's sister and her daughter.
    B. They are the mother and daughter from the rainstorm in Act One.
    C. They are former pupils of Higgins.
    D. They are tutors Higgins has hired to help Eliza.

18. Henry says, "We want two or three people. You'll do as well as anybody else." What does this statement tell us about him?
    A. He is not a careful researcher.
    B. He doesn't really care how his experiment turns out.
    C. He is rude to everyone and only thinks of his work and himself.
    D. He is grateful for his mother's cooperation.

19. What does Liza do wrong at Mrs. Higgins' home?
    A. She uses her sleeve for a napkin.
    B. She tells an odd story of her aunt's death using vulgar, though well-pronounced, language.
    C. She accidentally admits that she can't read.
    D. She talks about the price of flowers and reveals her true identity.

20. What does Clara think of Eliza?
    A. Clara is jealous of Eliza's popularity.
    B. Clara thinks Eliza is a fraud and thinks herself above the others because she can see through the masquerade.
    C. Clara thinks Eliza is too snobby and sophisticated.
    D. Clara wants to use Eliza's new small-talk and to imitate her.

21. Who is Nepommuck?
    A. He is a guest at the ambassador's reception, fluent in many languages, who claims Eliza is really a princess.
    B. He is the taxi driver. He recognizes Eliza and announces that she is a fraud.
    C. He is the host's son. He falls madly in love with Eliza.
    D. He is a colleague of the Professor's. He congratulates Higgins on his excellent work.

22. Is Eliza successful at the ambassador's reception?
    A. Yes, she is.
    B. No, she isn't.
    C. She says she is, but Doolittle says she isn't.
    D. She doesn't think so, but Doolittle does, so she lets him go on thinking his way.

Pygmalion Multiple Choice Study Questions Page 5

Act Four

23. What did Eliza do to Higgins when they returned home?
    A. She cursed him in her former dialect.
    B. She threw his slippers at him.
    C. She wrote him a letter telling him how she really felt.
    D. She thanked him and went quietly up to bed, where she cried herself to sleep.

24. What is Higgins' advice to Liza when he realizes she is upset?
    A. He tells her to take a hot bath and eat some chocolate.
    B. He tells her to talk to Mrs. Pearce.
    C. He tells her to straighten up and act upper class.
    D. He tells her to go to bed, have a little cry, and say her prayers.

25. How does Eliza feel now?
    A. She is delighted with her new identity.
    B. She is not sure what she wants to do next. She sees good and bad in both alternatives.
    C. She is angry at Higgins because she says she isn't fit now for anything but being a lady.
    D. She realizes that the upper class are a group of senseless snobs, and she wants to return to the streets she knows.

26. Why does Liza tell Freddy, "Don't you call me Miss Doolittle . . . Liza is good enough for me."?
    A. She feels in many ways that "Liza" in her old way was a better person than "Miss Doolittle."
    B. She still thinks of Freddy as her equal.
    C. She thinks he is being sarcastic, and she wants him to stop.
    D. She doesn't like using her father's name at all.

27. What was Freddy doing below Eliza's window?
    A. He was spying for her father.
    B. He was listening to see if he could learn anything from the Professor's lessons.
    C. He has fallen in love with her and hangs around hoping to get a glimpse of her.
    D. He was hoping she would want to take a ride and he could get some more business.

Pygmalion Multiple Choice Study Questions Page 6

Act Five

28. Why is Henry Higgins concerned about Liza's being gone?
    A. He is afraid that she will say things that will damage his reputation in the academic and social communities.
    B. Her absence has affected him personally. He misses her services; he can't find anything and doesn't know when his appointments are.
    C. He knows that he is legally responsible if anything happens to her, and he doesn't want to have to be involved with the police.
    D. He wants to use her in another experiment and is angry that he can't get started.

29. Why is Alfred Doolittle upset?
    A. He has unwillingly come into money and now has the responsibilities of being middle class.
    B. He really wants to marry someone other than the woman he is about to marry.
    C. He was hoping to get more money from Higgins.
    D. He has realized how much he misses Eliza, and he wants her to come home with him.

30. Higgins says, "She behaved in the most outrageous way. I never gave her the slightest provocation." Is he lying or not?
    A. Yes, he is. He realizes his mistakes but doesn't want to admit them.
    B. No, he isn't. He is blind to his own sensitivities.
    C. One can't really tell from the story.

31. What becomes of Eliza?
    A. She goes off with Nepommuck to tour Europe.
    B. She marries Freddy and runs her own flower shop.
    C. She stays with Higgins as his secretary.
    D. She goes on to the university to study with Pickering.

ANSWER KEY: MULTIPLE CHOICE STUDY/QUIZ QUESTIONS
Pygmalion

<u>Act One</u>
1. A
2. C
3. D
4. B
5. C
6. A

<u>Act Two</u>
7. B
8. B
9. A
10. C
11. C
12. C
13. C
14. B
15. C
16. B

<u>Act Three</u>
17. B
18. C
19. B
20. D
21. A
22. A

<u>Act Four</u>
23. B
24. D
25. C
26. A
27. C

<u>Act Five</u>
28. B
29. A
30. B
31. B

PREREADING VOCABULARY WORKSHEETS

VOCABULARY - *Pygmalion*

Act One

Part I: Using Prior Knowledge and Contextual Clues

Below are the sentences in which the vocabulary words appear in the text. Read the sentence. Use any clues you can find in the sentence combined with your prior knowledge, and write what you think the underlined words mean on the lines provided.

1. If Freddy had a bit of gumption, he would have got one at the theater door.

_____

2. She sits down on the plinth of the column, sorting her flowers.

_____

3. An elderly gentleman of the amiable military type rushes into the shelter, and closes a dripping umbrella.

_____

4. General hubbub, mostly sympathetic to the flower girl, but depreciating her excessive sensibility.

_____

5. Her daughter repudiates her with an angry shrug and retires haughtily.

_____

6. A woman who utters such depressing and disgusting sounds has no right to be anywhere . . . don't sit there crooning like a bilious pigeon.

_____

7. THE FLOWER GIRL: . . . Buy a flower, kind gentleman. I'm short for my lodging. . . .
   HIGGINS: [Shocked at the girl's mendacity]

_____

8. This prodigal mood does not extinguish her gnawing sense of the need for economy . . . .

_____

Pygmalion Vocabulary Worksheet Act One Continued

9. So she takes off her shawl and skirt and adds them to the <u>miscellaneous</u> bedclothes.

_____

Part II: Determining the Meaning: Match the vocabulary words to their dictionary definitions.

___ 1. gumption A. rejects the validity or authority of
___ 2. plinth B. belittling
___ 3. amiable C. begging
___ 4. depreciating D. a block or slab on which a pedestal, column or statue is placed
___ 5. repudiates E. boldness of enterprise; initiative or aggressiveness
___ 6. bilious F. having a variety of characteristics, abilities, or appearances
___ 7. mendacity G. rashly or wastefully extravagant
___ 8. prodigal H. friendly and agreeable
___ 9. miscellaneous I. appearing as if experiencing gastric distress caused by a disorder of the liver

Pygmalion Vocabulary Worksheet Acts Two and Three

Part I: Using Prior Knowledge and Contextual Clues

    Below are the sentences in which the vocabulary words appear in the text. Read the sentence. Use any clues you can find in the sentence combined with your prior knowledge, and write what you think the underlined words mean on the lines provided.

1. He is . . . rather like a very impetuous baby 'taking notice' eagerly and loudly, and requiring almost as much watching to keep him out of unintended mischief.

___

2. HIGGINS [peremptorily] Sit down.

___

3. Higgins, thus scolded, subsides. The hurricane is succeeded by a zephyr of amiable surprise.

___

4. PICKERING [in good-humored remonstrance] Does it occur to you, Higgins, that the girl has some feelings?

___

5. I want to change you from a frowzy slut to a clean, respectable girl fit to sit with the gentlemen in the study.

___

6. HIGGINS [dogmatically lifting himself on his hands to the level of the piano, and sitting on it with a bounce]

___

7. LIZA [speaking with pedantic correctness of pronunciation and great beauty of tone]

___

8. She is so intent on her ordeal that she walks like a somnambulist in a desert instead of a debutante in a fashionable crowd.

___

Pygmalion Vocabulary Worksheet Acts Two and Three Continued

Part II: Determining the Meaning: Match the vocabulary words to their dictionary definitions.

___ 10. impetuous   A. sloppy; slovenly
___ 11. peremptorily   B. by the book; following the rules exactly
___ 12. zephyr   C. sleepwalker
___ 13. remonstrance   D. characterized by an authoritative, arrogant assertion
___ 14. frowzy   E. impulsive and passionate
___ 15. dogmatically   F. an expression of protests, complaint or reproof
___ 16. pedantic   G. not allowing contradiction or refusal; commanding
___ 17. somnambulist   H. something that is airy, insubstantial or passing

Pygmalion Vocabulary Worksheet Acts Four and Five

Part I: Using Prior Knowledge and Contextual Clues
     Below are the sentences in which the vocabulary words appear in the text. Read the sentence. Use any clues you can find in the sentence combined with your prior knowledge, and write what you think the underlined words mean on the lines provided.

1. . . . I felt like a bear in a cage, hanging about doing nothing. The dinner was worse; sitting gorging there for over an hour, with nobody but a damned fool of a fashionable woman to talk to! I tell you, Pickering, never again for me! . . . The whole thing has been simple <u>purgatory</u>.

_____

2. He'll have you to pay for all those <u>togs</u> you have been wearing today . . . .

_____

3. Can I drive you and the lady anywhere, sir? They start <u>asunder</u>.

_____

4. HIGGINS: . . . Let her go. Let her find out how she can get on without us. She will relapse into the gutter in three weeks without me at her elbow. . . .
   PICKERING: He's <u>incorrigible</u>, Eliza. You won't relapse, will you?

_____

5. If the Colonel says I must, I--I'll [almost sobbing] I'll <u>demean</u> myself.

_____

6. I should indeed be honored by your <u>condescension</u>.

_____

7. You had better come to the <u>brougham</u> with me. Colonel Pickering can go with the bridegroom.

_____

Pygmalion Vocabulary Worksheet Acts Four and Five Continued

8. DOOLITTLE [sad but <u>magnanimous</u>] They played you off very cunning, Eliza, them two sportsmen.

_____

Part II: Determining the Meaning: Match the vocabulary words to their dictionary definitions.

___ 18. purgatory   A. to descend to the level of one considered inferior
___ 19. togs   B. apart from each other in position or direction
___ 20. asunder   C. clothes
___ 21. incorrigible   D. a closed four-wheeled carriage with an open driver's seat in front
___ 22. demean   E. courageously noble
___ 23. condescension   F. to humble oneself
___ 24. brougham   G. incapable of being corrected or reformed
___ 25. magnanimous   H. a place or condition of suffering, expiation or remorse

ANSWER KEY: VOCABULARY - *Pygmalion*

Act One
1. E
2. D
3. H
4. B
5. A
6. I
7. C
8. G
9. F

Acts Two and Three
10. E
11. G
12. H
13. F
14. A
15. D
16. B
17. C

Acts Four and Five

18. H
19. C
20. B
21. G
22. F
23. A
24. D
25. E

DAILY LESSONS

LESSON ONE

Objectives
    1. To introduce the *Pygmalion* unit.
    2. To distribute books and other related materials
    3. To introduce the project assignment
    4. To assign speaking parts for the reading of the play

NOTE: You need to have prepared a bulletin board titled: MOM SAYS, "MIND YOUR MANNERS" or some other appropriate title.

Activity #1
    Have a variety of markers available for students to use to write up things they've learned that make "good manners"--things like, "Don't burp at the table," "Say 'Please' and 'Thank you,'" "Don't tell Aunt Martha her special lasagna tastes awful," or "Thank Grandma for the pink bunny pajamas she got you for Christmas even though you hate them."

TRANSITION: Explain to students that they are going to read a play about a man who bets he can take a young woman from the streets--with no social graces--and pass her off as a duchess at an ambassador's garden party.

Activity #2
    Distribute the materials students will use in this unit. Explain in detail how students are to use these materials.

    Study Guides Students should read the study guide questions for each reading assignment prior to beginning the reading assignment to get a feeling for what events and ideas are important in the section they are about to read. After reading the section, students will (as a class or individually) answer the questions to review the important events and ideas from that section of the book. Students should keep the study guides as study materials for the unit test.

    Vocabulary Prior to reading a reading assignment, students will do vocabulary work related to the section of the book they are about to read. Following the completion of the reading of the book, there will be a vocabulary review of all the words used in the vocabulary assignments. Students should keep their vocabulary work as study materials for the unit test.

    Reading Assignment Sheet You need to fill in the reading assignment sheet to let students know by when their reading has to be completed. You can either write the assignment sheet up on a side blackboard or bulletin board and leave it there for students to see each day, or you can "ditto" copies for each student to have. In either case, you should advise students to become very familiar with the reading assignments so they know what is expected of them.

<u>Extra Activities Center</u> The resource pages of this unit contain suggestions for an extra library of related books and articles in your classroom as well as crossword and word search puzzles. Make an extra activities center in your room where you will keep these materials for students to use. (Bring the books and articles in from the library and keep several copies of the puzzles on hand.) Explain to students that these materials are available for students to use when they finish reading assignments or other class work early.

<u>Nonfiction Assignment Sheet</u> Explain to students that they each are to read at least one non-fiction piece from the in-class library at some time during the unit. Students will fill out a nonfiction assignment sheet after completing the reading to help you evaluate their reading experiences and to help the students think about and evaluate their own reading experiences.

<u>Books</u> Each school has its own rules and regulations regarding student use of school books. Advise students of the procedures that are normal for your school.

<u>Activity #3</u>
Distribute the Project Assignment sheets. Discuss the directions in detail.

<u>Activity #4</u>
Assign students speaking parts for the reading of the play. A parts assignment sheet is included for your convenience.

NONFICTION ASSIGNMENT SHEET
(To be completed after reading the required nonfiction article)

Name _____ Date _____

Title of Nonfiction Read _____

Written By _____ Publication Date _____

I. Factual Summary: Write a short summary of the piece you read.

II. Vocabulary
1. With which vocabulary words in the piece did you encounter some degree of difficulty?

2. How did you resolve your lack of understanding with these words?

III. Interpretation: What was the main point the author wanted you to get from reading his work?

IV. Criticism
1. With which points of the piece did you agree or find easy to accept? Why?

2. With which points of the piece did you disagree or find difficult to believe? Why?

V. Personal Response: What do you think about this piece? OR How does this piece influence your ideas?

PROJECT ASSIGNMENT - *Pygmalion*

PROMPT

In the play *Pygmalion*, Higgins bets he can pass Liza off as a duchess at a garden party, even though she is just a flower girl from the streets. Not many people get to go to formal garden parties anymore; people just don't have these kinds of events as much as they used to. Your assignment is to plan and actually have a formal garden party for your class.

GETTING STARTED

Your class has been (or will now be) divided into six groups, one group for each of the following assignments:

      Decorations
      Entertainment
      Invitations & Seating Arrangements (if necessary)
      Attire
      Menu
      Rules for Behavior at a Garden Party

Decorations - Your group is to find out what decorations are appropriate for a formal garden party, decide upon what decorations you want to use, and make sure the decorations are in place for the day of the party. You are also responsible for the removal of the decorations after the party is over.

Entertainment - Your group is responsible for finding out what entertainment is appropriate for a formal garden party, decide what kind of entertainment you will provide for your guests, and make sure the appropriate arrangements are made for the day of the party. You are also responsible for removal/return of anything used relating to the entertainment part of the party.

Invitations & Seating Arrangements - Your group is responsible for finding out what kinds of invitations are appropriate for a formal garden party, to create and send the invitations, to give a final head count to the menu group. Also find out whether or not seating arrangements are necessary, and if they are, take care of that detail.

Attire - Your group is responsible for finding out what people should wear to a formal garden party, making everyone aware of what is expected, and to be there on the day of the party to make sure all of your guests are appropriately attired.

Pygmalion Garden Party Project Page 2

Menu - Your group is responsible for finding out what should be served at a formal garden party, deciding upon a menu for the event, and making the necessary arrangements to see that the food and beverages are prepared for the day of the party. You are also responsible for cleaning up anything relating to food and beverages after the party is over.

Rules for Behavior - Your group is responsible for finding out how people should act at a garden party, letting everyone who is attending know what is expected of them, and for maintaining decorum on the day of the party.

IN ADDITION

In addition, all groups will be responsible for bringing whatever food/beverages/goods the menu group decides to assign for them to bring.

REQUIREMENTS

Each group must fill out a Project Worksheet which has the specific assignments for each student in the group.

Each person in the group must contribute to the group's efforts.

Everyone must participate in the manner appropriate for a formal garden party on the day of the party.

TIMETABLE

You are getting this project assignment now so you can begin to think about your plans. One day within the next week you will go to the library, at which time you may use the library resources to find out what you need to know and to begin making your plans as a group. You will be given one other class period to work on this project and coordinate your group's efforts. About a week after that, you will have your Garden Party Day.

PROJECT WORKSHEET - *Pygmalion*

Group Name _____

Group Members

_____   _____

_____   _____

_____   _____

Task To Be Done	Name of Person Doing It	Completion Date	Done?

SPEAKING PARTS ASSIGNMENTS - *Pygmalion*

Act One
Narrator (non-character parts)
Daughter
Mother
Bystander
Freddy
Flower Girl
Gentleman (Pickering)
Note Taker (Higgins)
Sarcastic Bystander
Taximan

Act Two
Narrator
Higgins
Pickering
Pearce
Flower Girl (Liza)
Doolittle

Act Three
Narrator
Mrs. Higgins
Higgins
Parlormaid
Mrs. Eynsford Hill
Pickering
Freddy
Miss Eynsford Hill (Clara)
Liza
Whiskers (Nepommuck)
Host
Hostess

Pygmalion Speaking Part Assignments Continued

Act Four
Narrator
Liza
Higgins
Freddy
Pickering
Constables
Taximan

Act Five
Narrator
Parlormaid
Mrs. Higgins
Higgins
Pickering
Doolittle
Liza

LESSON TWO

Objectives
    1. To preview the study questions and vocabulary for Act One
    2. To give students the opportunity to practice their speaking parts

Activity #1
    Give students about fifteen minutes to preview the study questions for Act One and to do the related vocabulary worksheet.

Activity #2
    When students finish their worksheets, they should begin practicing/reading over the speaking parts they were assigned.

LESSON THREE

Objectives
    1. To read Act One
    2. To evaluate students' oral reading
    3. To preview the study questions and vocabulary for Acts two and three

Activity #1
    Have students read the speaking parts they were assigned in Lesson Two. Try to finish reading through Act One during this class period if possible. If you have not yet completed an oral reading evaluation for your class this marking period, this would be a good opportunity to do so. An evaluation form follows for your convenience.

Activity #2
    Tell students that prior to the next class meeting they should have completed the prereading work for Acts two and three.

ORAL READING EVALUATION - *Pygmalion*

Name _____ Class____ Date _____

SKILL	EXCELLENT	GOOD	AVERAGE	FAIR	POOR
Fluency	5	4	3	2	1
Clarity	5	4	3	2	1
Audibility	5	4	3	2	1
Pronunciation	5	4	3	2	1
_____	5	4	3	2	1
_____	5	4	3	2	1

Total _____ Grade _____

Comments:

LESSON FOUR

Objectives
1. To review the main events and ideas from Act One
2. To read Act Two and Act Three
3. To preview the study questions and vocabulary words for Act Four and Act Five

Activity #1
Give students a few minutes to formulate answers for the study guide questions for Act One, and then discuss the answers to the questions in detail. Write the answers on the board or overhead transparency so students can have the correct answers for study purposes. NOTE: It is a good practice in public speaking and leadership skills for individual students to take charge of leading the discussions of the study questions. Perhaps a different student could go to the front of the class and lead the discussion each day that the study questions are discussed during this unit. Of course, the teacher should guide the discussion when appropriate and be sure to fill in any gaps the students leave.

Activity #2
Have students read the speaking parts they were assigned in Lesson Two. Continue the oral reading evaluations. Try to read through Act Three if possible.

Activity #3
Tell students that prior to your next class meeting they should preview the study questions for Act Four and Act Five of *Pygmalion* and to do the related vocabulary work.

LESSON FIVE

Objectives
1. To review the main ideas and events from Act Two and Act Three
2. To read Act Four and Act Five
3. To complete the oral reading evaluations

Activity #1
Give students a few minutes to formulate answers for the study guide questions for Act Two and Act Three, and then discuss the answers to the questions in detail. Write the answers on the board or overhead transparency so students can have the correct answers for study purposes.

Activity #2
Have students read the speaking parts they were assigned in Lesson Two. Complete the oral reading evaluations. Try to read through Act Five if possible.

LESSON SIX

Objectives
    1. To review the main ideas and events from Act Four and Act Five
    2. To discuss *Pygmalion* on interpretive and critical levels

Activity #1
    Take a few minutes at the beginning of the period to review the study questions for Act Four and Act Five.

Activity #2
    Choose the questions from the Extra Discussion Questions/Writing Assignments which seem most appropriate for your students. A class discussion of these questions is most effective if students have been given the opportunity to formulate answers to the questions prior to the discussion. To this end, you may either have all the students formulate answers to all the questions, divide your class into groups and assign one or more questions to each group, or you could assign one question to each student in your class. The option you choose will make a difference in the amount of class time needed for this activity.

Activity #3
    After students have had ample time to formulate answers to the questions, begin your class discussion of the questions and the ideas presented by the questions. Be sure students take notes during the discussion so they have information to study for the unit test.

EXTRA WRITING ASSIGNMENTS/DISCUSSION QUESTIONS - *Pygmalion*

Interpretation

1. What are the main conflicts in the play, and how is each resolved?

2. What does the setting add to the story?

3. Where is the climax of the play? Justify your answer.

4. Are the characters in the play stereotypes? If so, explain why stereotypes were used. If not, explain how the characters merit individuality.

5. Could anything have been gained by adding more scenes either before the beginning of the play or after the ending? If so, what and for what purpose? If not, why not?

Critical

6. Discuss the ideas by which Higgins lives his life. Do they have any merit?

7. Are Liza's actions believably motivated? Explain why or why not.

8. Compare and contrast Higgins and Pickering.

9. Characterize Bernard Shaw's style of writing. How does it contribute to the value of the play?

10. Compare and contrast Liza and Clara.

11. Compare and contrast Mrs. Higgins and Mrs. Eynsford Hill.

12. Who is responsible for Liza's situation? Explain why.

13. Explain how the title relates to the events of the play and the themes of *Pygmalion*.

14. Explain Pickering's role in the play. Why was he included?

15. What is Mrs. Pearce's role in the story? What is her use as a character?

16. Explain how the names of the characters are appropriate.

17. Is the story of *Pygmalion* believable? Explain why or why not.

18. Explain how Liza's view of "lady" changes during the course of the play.

19. Who is the main character of the play? Justify your answer.

Pygmalion Extra Discussion Questions page 2

Critical/Personal Response

20. Define "good girl" as you think Liza would.

21. Discuss the meaning of the following quotations in relationship to the themes of the play:
    a. "You and I and Pickering will be three old bachelors instead of only two men and a silly girl."
    b. "... the difference between a lady and a flower girl is not how she behaves, but how she is treated."
    c. "The question is not whether I treat you rudely, but whether you ever heard me treat anyone else better."
    d. "I care for life, for humanity; and you are a part of it that has come my way and been built into my house. What more can you or anyone ask?"
    e. "Making life means making trouble."
    f. "I only want to be natural."

Personal Response

25. Did you enjoy reading *Pygmalion*? Why or why not?

26. What is the difference between "being rich" and "having class"?

27. Eliza Doolittle aspired to work in a real flower shop instead of on the corner. Define and describe one of your aspirations.

28. Define "vulgar."

29. Have you read any other books or seen any movies that were similar in any way to *Pygmalion*? If so, what were they?

LESSON SEVEN

Objective
    To review all of the vocabulary work done in this unit

Activity
    Choose one (or more) of the vocabulary review activities listed below and spend your class period as directed in the activity. Some of the materials for these review activities are located in the Vocabulary Resource section of this unit.

VOCABULARY REVIEW ACTIVITIES

1. Divide your class into two teams and have an old-fashioned spelling or definition bee.

2. Give each of your students (or students in groups of two, three or four) a *Pygmalion* Vocabulary Word Search Puzzle. The person (group) to find all of the vocabulary words in the puzzle first wins.

3. Give students a *Pygmalion* Vocabulary Word Search Puzzle without the word list. The person or group to find the most vocabulary words in the puzzle wins.

4. Use a *Pygmalion* Vocabulary Crossword Puzzle. Put the puzzle onto a transparency on the overhead projector (so everyone can see it), and do the puzzle together as a class.

5. Give students a *Pygmalion* Vocabulary Matching Worksheet to do.

6. Divide your class into two teams. Use the *Pygmalion* vocabulary words with their letters jumbled as a word list. Student 1 from Team A faces off against Student 1 from Team B. You write the first jumbled word on the board. The first student (1A or 1B) to unscramble the word wins the chance for his/her team to score points. If 1A wins the jumble, go to student 2A and give him/her a definition. He/she must give you the correct spelling of the vocabulary word which fits that definition. If he/she does, Team A scores a point, and you give student 3A a definition for which you expect a correctly spelled matching vocabulary word. Continue giving Team A definitions until some team member makes an incorrect response. An incorrect response sends the game back to the jumbled-word face off, this time with students 2A and 2B. Instead of repeating giving definitions to the first few students of each team, continue with the student after the one who gave the last incorrect response on the team. For example, if Team B wins the jumbled-word face-off, and student 5B gave the last incorrect answer for Team B, you would start this round of definition questions with student 6B, and so on. The team with the most points wins!

7. Have students write a story in which they correctly use as many vocabulary words as possible. Have students read their compositions orally. Post the most original compositions on your bulletin board.

LESSON EIGHT

Objectives
> 1. To give students the opportunity to use the library's resources to help them in their projects
> 2. To give students time to plan their class projects

Activity

Take students to the library. Give them this class period to begin planning their Garden Party Day. Remind students that they must all read an article of nonfiction related to *Pygmalion* before this unit is over. They may use the reading they do for this project as their nonfiction reading if they choose. Remind them that they are to fill out a Nonfiction Assignment Sheet.

NOTE: If your school library does not have any information about social manners, you might go to your public library, check out appropriate information, and have it in your room for students to use. In that case, there would be no need to go to the library; students could work right in your room.

LESSON NINE

Objectives
> 1. To give students the opportunity to practice writing to inform
> 2. To evaluate students' research experiences
> 3. To give the teacher the opportunity to evaluate students' writing skills
> 4. To help students review and summarize the information they read about in the last class period

Activity

Distribute Writing Assignment #1. Discuss the directions in detail and give students ample time to complete the assignment.

LESSON TEN

Objective
> To give students time to coordinate their group work for the class project

Activity

Give students this class period to coordinate their group work for the Garden Party project. Students should be finished with their research, have made the bulk of their plans, and should now need to coordinate with other groups and make final preparations for the event.

WRITING ASSIGNMENT #1 - *Pygmalion*

PROMPT
You have done most of your research for the class project. Take a minute now to review and summarize your research. Your assignment is to write a composition in which you explain what research you did and what you found out.

PREWRITING
Most of your prewriting has been done already in the form of the notes you took while you were reading. Just take a minute now to organize and review your notes (or jot down what you remember about what you read if you didn't take any notes) and organize the information you have.

DRAFTING
Write a paragraph in which you introduce your topic and explain what you were researching.
In the body of your composition, tell what you found out as you read. Write at least three paragraphs, using as much detail as possible.
Write a concluding paragraph in which you determine if the information you found was sufficient or if you will need to do more research to get the information you need.

PROMPT
When you finish the rough draft of your paper, ask a student who sits near you to read it. After reading your rough draft, he/she should tell you what he/she liked best about your work, which parts were difficult to understand, and ways in which your work could be improved. Reread your paper considering your critic's comments and make the corrections you think are necessary.

PROOFREADING
Do a final proofreading of your paper double-checking your grammar, spelling, organization, and the clarity of your ideas.

LESSONS ELEVEN AND TWELVE

Objectives
1. To show students a film version of the play
2. To give students an example to follow for what a garden party should be
3. To show students how to act with social manners when they may need to do so

Activity
Use these class periods to show students the film or video of *My Fair Lady*.

LESSON THIRTEEN

Objectives
1. To give students the opportunity to practice writing to persuade
2. To review the character traits of Liza and Higgins
3. To give the teacher the opportunity to evaluate students' writing

Activity
Distribute Writing Assignment #2. Discuss the directions in detail and give students ample time to complete the assignment.

LESSON FOURTEEN

Objectives
1. To widen the breadth of students' knowledge about the topics discussed or touched upon in *Pygmalion*
2. To check students' nonfiction reading assignments

Activity
Ask each student to give a brief oral report about the nonfiction work he/she read for the nonfiction reading assignment. Your criteria for evaluating this report will vary depending on the level of your students. You may wish for students to give a complete report without using notes of any kind, or you may want students to read directly from a written report, or you may want to do something in between these two extremes. Just make students aware of your criteria in ample time for them to prepare their reports.

Start with one student's report. After that, ask if anyone else in the class has read on a topic related to the first student's report. If no one has, choose another student at random. After each report, be sure to ask if anyone has a report related to the one just completed. That will help keep a continuity during the discussion of the reports.

WRITING ASSIGNMENT #2 - *Pygmalion*

PROMPT
In class we have discussed Higgins' treatment of Liza. Your assignment is to convince Higgins that he should treat Liza better than he does. Write a composition as if you were talking to Higgins.

PREWRITING
Make a few notes. First, write down a list of words that describe how Higgins treats Liza. Next, write down a list of words that describe how he *should* treat her. Make a list of reasons why Higgins treats Liza the way he does. Finally, make a list of reasons why Higgins should treat Liza better.

DRAFTING
Write an introductory paragraph in which you bring up the subject of how Higgins treats Liza and introduce the idea that you think he should treat her better than he does.

In the body of your argument (composition), write at least three paragraphs, one paragraph for each of three reasons why Higgins should treat Liza better. Use a topic sentence for each paragraph telling the reason and then fill in the paragraphs with examples and explanations.

Write a concluding paragraph, a paragraph in which you state what your final words on the subject would be to Higgins.

PROMPT
When you finish the rough draft of your paper, ask a student who sits near you to read it. After reading your rough draft, he/she should tell you what he/she liked best about your work, which parts were difficult to understand, and ways in which your work could be improved. Reread your paper considering your critic's comments and make the corrections you think are necessary.

PROOFREADING
Do a final proofreading of your paper double-checking your grammar, spelling, organization, and the clarity of your ideas.

LESSON FIFTEEN

Objective
   To conclude the class project

Activity
   Have students prepare and attend your garden party.

   NOTE: Most of the details of the party have been left to you and your students. Each school has different rules, and each group of students has different capabilities. Whether you have an all-day affair, hold the party on or off school grounds or during or after school hours, and the list of "others" you will invite (besides your class) has been left up to you. Whatever the specific details you have decided upon, it should be a fun, educational experience for your students.

LESSON SIXTEEN

Objectives
   1. To give students the opportunity to express their personal opinions
   2. To get students to consider how important good manners are in their lives
   3. To give the teacher the opportunity to evaluate students' writing skills

Activity #1
   Distribute Writing Assignment #3. Discuss the directions in detail and give students ample time to complete the assignment.

Activity #2
   While students are working on Writing Assignment #3, call individual students to your desk or some other private area to discuss their writing skills. An evaluation form has been included in this unit for your convenience. Use the first two writing assignments of this unit as a basis for your evaluation conference.
   Students should revise at least one (preferably both) of their previous compositions taking into consideration your remarks. Give students a day and a date when these revisions will be due.
   When the revisions are handed in, use an A-C-E scale of grading: A=all corrections made, C=some corrections made, E=no corrections made. That will give students sufficient feedback and credit for their work, and yet it will speed your grading time considerably. Additional comments to the students and from the students to you are extremely helpful.

WRITING ASSIGNMENT #3 - *Pygmalion*

PROMPT

Eliza took all the trouble to learn about social graces and proper speech and decided that perhaps she was better off not knowing about such things, that perhaps she was a better person just as Liza instead of Miss Doolittle. If no one had any manners, people would live like pigs and would probably be fighting with each other all the time. On the other hand, one can't be too sure how terribly important it is with which fork one eats one's salad. Your assignment is to write a composition explaining how one decides what manners are important and which are somewhat frivolous.

PREWRITING

Make a list of all the reasons society needs people to have manners. Make a list of the kinds of manners that are most important to have.

DRAFTING

Write a paragraph in which you introduce the idea that society does need people to have manners but that perhaps some kinds of manners are more important for people to have than others.

In the body of your composition, write one paragraph for each reason why people should have manners and fill out your paragraph with examples to explain your point.

Also in the body of your composition write one paragraph explaining what kinds of manners or social graces are somewhat frivolous. Use examples to explain your point.

In conclusion write a paragraph in which you explain how a person is to know which manners are important and which ones are not.

PROMPT

When you finish the rough draft of your paper, ask a student who sits near you to read it. After reading your rough draft, he/she should tell you what he/she liked best about your work, which parts were difficult to understand, and ways in which your work could be improved. Reread your paper considering your critic's comments and make the corrections you think are necessary.

PROOFREADING

Do a final proofreading of your paper double-checking your grammar, spelling, organization, and the clarity of your ideas.

WRITING EVALUATION FORM - *Pygmalion*

Name _____ Date _____

    Grade _____

Circle One For Each Item:

Grammar:	excellent	good	average	poor
Spelling:	excellent	good	average	poor
Punctuation:	excellent	good	average	poor
Legibility:	excellent	good	average	poor

Strengths:

Weaknesses:

Comments/Suggestions:

LESSON SEVENTEEN

<u>Objective</u>
 To review the main ideas presented in *Pygmalion*

<u>Activity #1</u>
 Choose one of the review games/activities included in this guide and spend your class period as outlined there. Some materials for these activities are located in the Extra Activities section of this unit.

<u>Activity #2</u>
 Remind students that the Unit Test will be in the next class meeting. Stress the review of the Study Guides and their class notes as a last-minute, brush-up review for homework.

REVIEW GAMES/ACTIVITIES - *Pygmalion*

1. Ask the class to make up a unit test for *Pygmalion*. The test should have 4 sections: matching, true/false, short answer, and essay. Students may use 1/2 period to make the test and then swap papers and use the other 1/2 class period to take a test a classmate has devised (open book). You may want to use the unit test included in this guide or take questions from the students' unit tests to formulate your own test.

2. Take 1/2 period for students to make up true and false questions (including the answers). Collect the papers and divide the class into two teams. Draw a big tick-tack-toe board on the chalk board. Make one team X and one team O. Ask questions to each side, giving each student one turn. If the question is answered correctly, that students' team's letter (X or O) is placed in the box. If the answer is incorrect, no mark is placed in the box. The object is to get three marks in a row like tick-tack-toe. You may want to keep track of the number of games won for each team.

3. Take 1/2 period for students to make up questions (true/false and short answer). Collect the questions. Divide the class into two teams. You'll alternate asking questions to individual members of teams A & B (like in a spelling bee). The question keeps going from A to B until it is correctly answered, then a new question is asked. A correct answer does not allow the team to get another question. Correct answers are +2 points; incorrect answers are -1 point.

4. Have students pair up and quiz each other from their study guides and class notes.

5. Give students a *Pygmalion* crossword puzzle to complete.

6. Divide your class into two teams. Use the *Pygmalion* crossword words with their letters jumbled as a word list. Student 1 from Team A faces off against Student 1 from Team B. You write the first jumbled word on the board. The first student (1A or 1B) to unscramble the word wins the chance for his/her team to score points. If 1A wins the jumble, go to student 2A and give him/her a clue. He/she must give you the correct word which matches that clue. If he/she does, Team A scores a point, and you give student 3A a clue for which you expect another correct response. Continue giving Team A clues until some team member makes an incorrect response. An incorrect response sends the game back to the jumbled-word face off, this time with students 2A and 2B. Instead of repeating giving clues to the first few students of each team, continue with the student after the one who gave the last incorrect response on the team. For example, if Team B wins the jumbled-word face-off, and student 5B gave the last incorrect answer for Team B, you would start this round of clue questions with student 6B, and so on. The team with the most points wins!

UNIT TESTS

SHORT ANSWER UNIT TEST 1 - *Pygmalion*

I. Matching/Identify

____ 1. Ambassador   A. Liza's last name

____ 2. Clara   B. Housekeeper for Higgins

____ 3. Doolittle   C. He transforms Eliza

____ 4. Eynsford   D. Author

____ 5. Freddy   E. Flower girl who becomes a lady

____ 6. Higgins   F. He had a reception/garden party

____ 7. Liza   G. ___ Hill; mother and daughter

____ 8. Nepommuck   H. The Colonel

____ 9. Pearce   I. She tries to imitate Liza

____ 10. Pickering   J. He created a statue of a woman so beautiful he fell in love with her

____ 11. Pygmalion   K. Guest at the party who was fluent in many languages

____ 12. Shaw   L. Eliza marries him

II. Short Answer

1. What purpose does the rain shower in the first act serve?

2. The note taker brags about what he could do for the flower girl within three months. What does he claim?

3. Why does Doolittle want only five pounds instead of the ten he is offered?

Pygmalion Short Answer Unit Test 1, Page 2

4. What does Liza do wrong at Mrs. Higgins' house?

5. What does Clara think of Eliza?

6. Why did Eliza throw Higgins' slippers at him?

7. Why does Liza tell Freddy, "Don't you call me Miss Doolittle . . . Liza is good enough for me"?

8. Why is Henry Higgins concerned about Liza's being gone?

9. What becomes of Eliza?

10. Explain how the title relates to the play.

Pygmalion Short Answer Unit Test 1 Page 3

III. Composition

What is the point of *Pygmalion*? When we read books, we usually come away from our reading experience a little richer, having given more thought to a particular aspect of life. What do you think Bernard Shaw intended us to gain from reading his play?

IV. Vocabulary

Listen to the vocabulary words and write them down.
Go back later and fill in the correct definition for each word.

1.

2.

3.

4.

5.

6.

7.

8.

9.

10.

SHORT ANSWER UNIT TEST 2 - *Pygmalion*

I. Matching

____ 1. Ambassador   A. The Colonel

____ 2. Clara   B. She tries to imitate Liza

____ 3. Doolittle   C. He created a statue of a woman so beautiful he fell in love with her

____ 4. Eynsford   D. Guest at the party who was fluent in many languages

____ 5. Freddy   E. Eliza marries him

____ 6. Higgins   F. ___ Hill; mother and daughter

____ 7. Liza   G. He had a reception/garden party

____ 8. Nepommuck   H. Liza's last name

____ 9. Pearce   I. Housekeeper for Higgins

____ 10. Pickering   J. He transforms Eliza

____ 11. Pygmalion   K. Author

____ 12. Shaw   L. Flower girl who becomes a lady

II. Short Answer

1. Under what circumstances do the characters in the play meet?

2. The note taker brags about what he could do for the flower girl within three months. What does he claim?

3. What does Eliza Doolittle want from Higgins?

Pygmalion Short Answer Unit Test 2 Page 2

4. Doolittle says, "I'm undeserving, and I mean to go on being undeserving." Why does he not want to better himself?

5. What does Liza do wrong at Mrs. Higgins' home?

6. "[At the corner of Trottenham Court] I sold flowers. I didn't sell myself. Now you've made a lady of me I'm not fit to sell anything else." Why did Liza say that?

III. Composition
1. Compare and contrast Higgins and Pickering.

2. Compare and contrast Liza and Clara.

Pygmalion Short Answer Unit Test 2 Page 3

3. Who is the main character in the play? Justify your answer.

4. ". . . the difference between a lady and a flower girl is not how she behaves, but how she's treated." Explain using examples from *Pygmalion*.

5. Why is Doolittle's name appropriate for him?

Pygmalion Short Answer Unit Test 2 Page 4

IV. Vocabulary

Listen to the vocabulary words and write them down.
Go back later and fill in the correct definition for each word.

1.

2.

3.

4.

5.

6.

7.

8.

9.

10.

KEY: SHORT ANSWER UNIT TESTS *Pygmalion*

The short answer questions are taken directly from the study guides.
If you need to look up the answers, you will find them in the study guide section.

Answers to the composition questions will vary depending on your
class discussions and the level of your students.

For the vocabulary section of the test, choose ten of the
words from the vocabulary lists to read orally for your students.

The answers to the matching section of the test are below.

Answers to the matching section of the Advanced Short Answer Unit Test
are the same as for Short Answer Unit Test #2.

Test #1	Test #2
1. F	1. G
2. I	2. B
3. A	3. H
4. G	4. F
5. L	5. E
6. C	6. J
7. E	7. L
8. K	8. D
9. B	9. I
10. H	10. A
11. J	11. C
12. D	12. K

ADVANCED SHORT ANSWER UNIT TEST - *Pygmalion*

I. Matching

____ 1. Ambassador   A. The Colonel

____ 2. Clara   B. She tries to imitate Liza

____ 3. Doolittle   C. He created a statue of a woman so beautiful he fell in love with her

____ 4. Eynsford   D. Guest at the party who was fluent in many languages

____ 5. Freddy   E. Eliza marries him

____ 6. Higgins   F. ___ Hill; mother and daughter

____ 7. Liza   G. He had a reception/garden party

____ 8. Nepommuck   H. Liza's last name

____ 9. Pearce   I. Housekeeper for Higgins

____ 10. Pickering   J. He transforms Eliza

____ 11. Pygmalion   K. Author

____ 12. Shaw   L. Flower girl who becomes a lady

II. Short Answer

1. By what ideas does Higgins live his life? Do they have any merit?

2. Explain how Liza's view of a "lady" changes throughout the course of the play.

3. Who is the main character in the play. Justify your answer.

Pygmalion Advanced Short Answer Unit Test Page 2

4. Compare and contrast Higgins and Pickering.

5. Compare and contrast Liza and Clara.

6. "The question is not whether I treat you rudely, but whether you have heard me treat anyone else better." Explain this line.

7. "Making life means making trouble." Explain the significance of this line in relation to the play.

8. ". . . the difference between a lady and a flower girl is not how she behaves, but how she's treated." Explain.

9. What does Liza learn by the end of the play?

Pygmalion Advanced Short Answer Unit Test Page 3

III. Composition

"His plays can scarcely prove other than lastingly delightful since they are the product of vigorous intelligence joined to inexhaustible comic invention." Explain how *Pygmalion* shows these traits said about George Bernard Shaw.

IV. Vocabulary

Write down the vocabulary words you are given. Go back later and use all of those vocabulary words in a composition relating to *Pygmalion*.

MULTIPLE CHOICE UNIT TEST 1 - *Pygmalion*

I. Matching

____ 1. Ambassador   A. Liza's last name

____ 2. Clara   B. Housekeeper for Higgins

____ 3. Doolittle   C. He transforms Eliza

____ 4. Eynsford   D. Author

____ 5. Freddy   E. Flower girl who becomes a lady

____ 6. Higgins   F. He had a reception/garden party

____ 7. Liza   G. ___ Hill; mother and daughter

____ 8. Nepommuck   H. The Colonel

____ 9. Pearce   I. She tries to imitate Liza

____ 10. Pickering   J. He created a statue of a woman so beautiful he fell in love with her

____ 11. Pygmalion   K. Guest at the party who was fluent in many languages

____ 12. Shaw   L. Eliza marries him

II. Multiple Choice

1. What purpose does the rain shower serve?
    A. It gives the main characters a relatively believable circumstance under which to meet.
    B. It symbolizes a washing away of old circumstances.
    C. It helps set up the conflict of man vs. nature.
    D. It shows that no one can control the weather. All, regardless of social station, are subject to it.

2. The note taker brags about what he could do for the flower girl within three months. What does he claim?
    A. He claims that he could get her into a good university.
    B. He claims that he could pass her off as a duchess at an ambassador's garden party.
    C. He claims that he could teach her to speak three languages fluently.
    D. He claims he could have her married to a wealthy member of high society.

Pygmalion Multiple Choice Test 1 Page 2

3. What do Higgins and Pickering have in common?
    A. They both study speech.
    B. They both went to Cambridge University.
    C. They both hate women.
    D. They both belong to the same church.

4. What does Eliza Doolittle want?
    A. She wants to marry Professor Higgins and get away from her terrible life.
    B. She wants to learn how to speak well enough to be able to work in a flower shop.
    C. She wants to get medical assistance for her lingering cough.
    D. She wants money so she can leave the city and start a new life.

5. Describe Mrs. Pearce's role.
    A. She acts like the mother Eliza never had.
    B. She adds an air of mystery, as the audience is never certain of her relationship with Higgins.
    C. She tries to be the voice of reason.
    D. She is a symbolic reminder of the next class upward from Eliza in English society.

6. Why did Alfred Doolittle come to see Professor Higgins?
    A. He wanted to ask Higgins to also teach his other two children.
    B. He wanted to blackmail Higgins to get some money for himself.
    C. He wanted to force Higgins to marry her.
    D. He wanted to wish Eliza good luck and bring her clothes to her.

7. Doolittle says, "I'm undeserving, and I mean to go on being undeserving."
   Why does he not want to better himself?
    A. He doesn't want to lose his friends.
    B. His belief in the class system is so firm that he is afraid to become better.
    C. He wants to have a life free from responsibilities and people's expectations.
    D. He doesn't believe he will be able to keep the money, and he doesn't want to get used to having it and then be disappointed.

8. Why does Doolittle want only five pounds instead of the ten he is offered?
    A. He doesn't think Eliza is worth ten pounds.
    B. He thinks if he asks for less now he will be in a better position later to get more.
    C. He doesn't know how to make change for anything over a five pound note.
    D. His wife told him to ask for five, and he always does what she says.

Pygmalion Multiple Choice Unit Test 1 Page 3

9. What does Liza do wrong at Mrs. Higgins' home?
    A. She uses her sleeve for a napkin.
    B. She tells an odd story of her aunt's death using vulgar, though well-pronounced, language.
    C. She accidentally admits that she can't read.
    D. She talks about the price of flowers, and reveals her true identity.

10. What does Clara think of Eliza?
    A. Clara is jealous of Eliza's popularity.
    B. Clara thinks Eliza is a fraud, and thinks herself above the others because she can see through the masquerade.
    C. Clara thinks Eliza is too snobby and sophisticated.
    D. Clara wants to use Eliza's new small-talk and to imitate her.

11. Why does Liza tell Freddy, "Don't you call me Miss Doolittle...Liza is good enough for me."?
    A. She feels in many ways that "Liza" in her old way was a better person than "Miss Doolittle."
    B. She still thinks of Freddy as her equal.
    C. She thinks he is being sarcastic, and she wants him to stop.
    D. She doesn't like using her father's name at all.

12. Why is Alfred Doolittle upset?
    A. He has unwillingly come into money and now has the responsibilities of being middle class.
    B. He really wants to marry someone other than the woman he is about to marry.
    C. He was hoping to get more money from Higgins.
    D. He has realized how much he misses Eliza; he wants her to come home with him.

13. What becomes of Eliza?
    A. She goes off with Nepommuck to tour Europe.
    B. She marries Freddy and runs her own flower shop.
    C. She stays with Higgins as his secretary.
    D. She goes on to the university to study with Pickering.

Pygmalion Multiple Choice Unit Test 1 Page 4

III. Composition

    Bernard Shaw wrote *Pygmalion* in 1912, and here we are reading it so many years later. Why? What makes this book a "classic"?

Pygmalion Multiple Choice Unit Test 1 Page 5

IV. Vocabulary

___ 1. Plinth   a. Courageously noble

___ 2. Magnanimous   b. By the book; following the rules exactly

___ 3. Somnambulist   c. Rejects the validity or authority of

___ 4. Purgatory   d. Apart from each other in position or direction

___ 5. Miscellaneous   e. Friendly and agreeable

___ 6. Remonstrance   f. Characterized by an authoritative, arrogant assertion of unproved or unprovable principles

___ 7. Incorrigible   g. A place or condition of suffering, expiation or remorse

___ 8. Peremptorily   h. Appearing as if experiencing gastric distress caused by a disorder of the liver

___ 9. Frowzy   i. Belittling

___ 10. Amiable   j. A closed four-wheeled carriage with an open driver's seat in front

___ 11. Repudiates   k. Sloppy; slovenly

___ 12. Togs   l. Incapable of being corrected or reformed

___ 13. Pedantic   m. A block or slab on which a pedestal, column or statue is placed

___ 14. Prodigal   n. Boldness or enterprise; initiative or aggressiveness

___ 15. Brougham   o. Not allowing contradiction or refusal; commanding

___ 16. Depreciating   p. An expression of protest, complaint or reproof

___ 17. Asunder   q. Sleepwalker

___ 18. Dogmatically   r. Clothes

___ 19. Bilious   s. Rashly or wastefully extravagant

___ 20. Gumption   t. Having a variety of characteristics, abilities, or appearances

MULTIPLE CHOICE UNIT TEST 2 - *Pygmalion*

I. Matching

____ 1. Ambassador   A. The Colonel

____ 2. Clara   B. She tries to imitate Liza

____ 3. Doolittle   C. He created a statue of a woman so beautiful he fell in love with her

____ 4. Eynsford   D. Guest at the party who was fluent in many languages

____ 5. Freddy   E. Eliza marries him

____ 6. Higgins   F. ___ Hill; mother and daughter

____ 7. Liza   G. He had a reception/garden party

____ 8. Nepommuck   H. Liza's last name

____ 9. Pearce   I. Housekeeper for Higgins

____ 10. Pickering   J. He transforms Eliza

____ 11. Pygmalion   K. Author

____ 12. Shaw   L. Flower girl who becomes a lady

II. Multiple Choice

1. What purpose does the rain shower serve?
   A. It shows that no one can control the weather; all, regardless of social station, are subject to it.
   B. It symbolizes a washing away of old circumstances.
   C. It helps the audience relate to the play, as the area where it was first performed was very rainy.
   D. It gives the main characters a relatively believable circumstance under which to meet.

2. The note taker brags about what he could do for the flower girl within three months. What does he claim?
   A. He claims that he could pass her off as a duchess at an ambassador's garden party.
   B. He claims that he could get her into a good university.
   C. He claims that he could teach her to speak three languages fluently.
   D. He claims he could have her married to a wealthy member of high society.

Pygmalion Multiple Choice Test 2 Page 2

3. What do Higgins and Pickering have in common?
    A. They both hate women.
    B. They both went to Cambridge University.
    C. They both study speech.
    D. All of the above

4. What does Eliza Doolittle want?
    A. She wants to marry Professor Higgins and get away from her terrible life.
    B. She wants money so she can leave the city and start a new life.
    C. She wants to get medical assistance for her lingering cough.
    D. She wants to learn how to speak well enough to be able to work in a flower shop.

5. Describe Mrs. Pearce's role.
    A. She acts like the mother Eliza never had.
    B. She tries to be the voice of reason.
    C. She adds an air of mystery, as the audience is never certain of her relationship with Higgins.
    D. She is a symbolic reminder of the next class upward from Eliza in English society.

6. Why did Alfred Doolittle come to see Professor Higgins?
    A. He wanted to blackmail Higgins to get some money for himself.
    B. He wanted to ask Higgins to also teach his other two children.
    C. He wanted to force Higgins to marry her.
    D. He wanted to wish Eliza good luck and bring her clothes to her.

7. Doolittle says, "I'm undeserving, and I mean to go on being undeserving." Why does he not want to better himself?
    A. He doesn't want to lose his friends.
    B. His belief in the class system is so firm that he is afraid to become better.
    C. He doesn't believe he will be able to keep the money, and he doesn't want to get used to having it and then be disappointed.
    D. He wants to have a life free from responsibilities and people's expectations.

8. Why does Doolittle want only five pounds instead of the ten he is offered?
    A. He doesn't think Eliza is worth ten pounds.
    B. He doesn't know how to make change for anything over a five pound note.
    C. He thinks if he asks for less now he will be in a better position later to get more.
    D. His wife told him to ask for five, and he always does what she says.

Pygmalion Multiple Choice Unit Test 2 Page 3

9. What does Liza do wrong at Mrs. Higgins' home?
    A. She tells an odd story of her aunt's death using vulgar, though well-pronounced, language.
    B. She uses her sleeve for a napkin.
    C. She accidentally admits that she can't read.
    D. She talks about the price of flowers and reveals her true identity.

10. What does Clara think of Eliza?
    A. Clara wants to use Eliza's new small-talk and to imitate her.
    B. Clara thinks Eliza is a fraud and thinks herself above the others because she can see through the masquerade.
    C. Clara thinks Eliza is too snobby and sophisticated.
    D. Clara is jealous of Eliza's popularity.

11. Why does Liza tell Freddy, "Don't you call me Miss Doolittle...Liza is good enough for me."?
    A. She still thinks of Freddy as her equal.
    B. She feels in many ways that "Liza" in her old way was a better person than "Miss Doolittle."
    C. She thinks he is being sarcastic, and she wants him to stop.
    D. She doesn't like using her father's name at all.

12. Why is Alfred Doolittle upset?
    A. He has realized how much he misses Eliza; he wants her to come home with him.
    B. He really wants to marry someone other than the woman he is about to marry.
    C. He was hoping to get more money from Higgins.
    D. He has unwillingly come into money and now has the responsibilities of being middle class.

13. What becomes of Eliza?
    A. She goes off with Nepommuck to tour Europe.
    B. She stays with Higgins as his secretary.
    C. She marries Freddy and runs her own flower shop.
    D. She goes on to the university to study with Pickering.

III. Composition
> Describe the relationship between Higgins and Eliza from the beginning of the play to the end.

Pygmalion Multiple Choice Unit Test 2 Page 5

IV. Vocabulary

___ 1. Frowzy   a. Clothes

___ 2. Peremptorily   b. A block or slab on which a pedestal, column or statue is placed

___ 3. Condescension   c. Belittling

___ 4. Pedantic   d. Incapable of being corrected or reformed

___ 5. Togs   e. A closed four-wheeled carriage with an open driver's seat in front

___ 6. Brougham   f. Something that is airy, insubstantial or passing

___ 7. Bilious   g. Appearing as if experiencing gastric distress caused by a disorder of the liver

___ 8. Somnambulist   h. By the book; following the rules exactly

___ 9. Demean   i. To descend to the level of one considered inferior

___ 10. Zephyr   j. An expression of protest, complaint or reproof

___ 11. Incorrigible   k. Not allowing contradiction or refusal; commanding

___ 12. Amiable   l. Friendly and agreeable

___ 13. Depreciating   m. To humble oneself

___ 14. Remonstrance   n. Apart from each other in position or direction

___ 15. Repudiates   o. Sloppy; slovenly

___ 16. Impetuous   p. Begging

___ 17. Plinth   q. A place or condition of suffering, expiation or remorse

___ 18. Asunder   r. Sleepwalker

___ 19. Purgatory   s. Impulsive and passionate

___ 20. Mendacity   t. Rejects the validity or authority of

ANSWER SHEET - *Pygmalion*
Multiple Choice Unit Tests

I. Matching
1. ___
2. ___
3. ___
4. ___
5. ___
6. ___
7. ___
8. ___
9. ___
10. ___
11. ___
12. ___

II. Multiple Choice
1. ___
2. ___
3. ___
4. ___
5. ___
6. ___
7. ___
8. ___
9. ___
10. ___
11. ___
12. ___
13. ___

IV. Vocabulary
1. ___
2. ___
3. ___
4. ___
5. ___
6. ___
7. ___
8. ___
9. ___
10. ___
11. ___
12. ___
13. ___
14. ___
15. ___
16. ___
17. ___
18. ___
19. ___
20. ___

ANSWER KEY - *Pygmalion*
Multiple Choice Unit Tests

Answers to Unit Test 1 are in the left column. Answers to Unit Test 2 are in the right column.

I. Matching		II. Multiple Choice		IV. Vocabulary	
1. F	G	1. A	D	1. M	O
2. I	B	2. B	A	2. A	K
3. A	H	3. A	C	3. Q	I
4. G	F	4. B	D	4. G	H
5. L	E	5. C	B	5. T	A
6. C	J	6. B	A	6. P	E
7. E	L	7. C	D	7. L	G
8. K	D	8. B	C	8. O	R
9. B	I	9. B	A	9. K	M
10. H	A	10. D	A	10. E	F
11. J	C	11. A	B	11. C	D
12. D	K	12. A	D	12. R	L
		13. B	C	13. B	C
				14. S	J
				15. J	T
				16. I	S
				17. D	B
				18. F	N
				19. H	Q
				20. N	P

UNIT RESOURCE MATERIALS

BULLETIN BOARD IDEAS - *Pygmalion*

1. Save one corner of the board for the best of students' *Pygmalion* writing assignments.

2. Take one of the word search puzzles from the extra activities section and with a marker copy it over in a large size on the bulletin board. Write the clue words to find to one side. Invite students prior to and after class to find the words and circle them on the bulletin board.

3. Write several of the most significant quotations from the book onto the board on brightly colored paper.

4. Make a bulletin board listing the vocabulary words for this unit. As you complete sections of the play and discuss the vocabulary for each section, write the definitions on the bulletin board. (If your board is one students face frequently, it will help them learn the words.)

5. Do a bulletin board about phonetics. Find passages from books or plays where the author has tried to represent a particular dialect. Write them up on the board. Perhaps you could find a good general explanation or at least definition of phonetics to include on the board.

6. Do a bulletin board about the legend of Pygmalion. If you are not artistic, perhaps you could find an art student at your school to illustrate the story.

7. This is a great time to do a fun bulletin board about tips from "Miss Manners." If you don't like the introductory activity, letting the students put up the tips they've gotten over the years, find a Miss Manners book and write down a few of your own favorites.

8. Make a bulletin board about famous people who started out with nothing. Post their pictures and do a little write-up about each one. (This would also make a good assignment.)

9. Make a bulletin board about the study of the effects of heredity versus environment. (A movie, *Trading Places*, was made about that topic several years ago. Two rich, old men bet a dollar against each other that one can take a person off of the street and turn him into a successful businessman. You might preview the movie to see if it is appropriate for your class.)

10. Post pictures from a production of the play.

EXTRA ACTIVITIES

One of the difficulties in teaching a play is that all students don't read at the same speed. One student who likes to read may take the book home and finish it in a day or two. Sometimes a few students finish the in-class assignments early. The problem, then, is finding suitable extra activities for students.

The best thing I've found is to keep a little library in the classroom. For this unit on *Pygmalion,* you might check out from the school library other related books and articles about manners, social graces, lifestyles of the rich, lifestyles of the poor, agencies that are willing to help people who want help with improving their lives, phonetics, and critics' articles about the play. Other plays by Bernard Shaw would be good to have on hand, too.

Other things you may keep on hand are puzzles. We have made some relating directly to *Pygmalion* for you. Feel free to duplicate them.

Some students may like to draw. You might devise a contest or allow some extra-credit grade for students who draw characters or scenes from *Pygmalion*. Note, too, that if the students do not want to keep their drawings you may pick up some extra bulletin board materials this way. If you have a contest and you supply the prize (a CD or something like that perhaps), you could, possibly, make the drawing itself a non-returnable entry fee.

The pages which follow contain games, puzzles and worksheets. The keys, when appropriate, immediately follow the puzzle or worksheet. There are two main groups of activities: one group for the unit; that is, generally relating to the *Pygmalion* text, and another group of activities related strictly to the *Pygmalion* vocabulary.

Directions for these games, puzzles and worksheets are self-explanatory. The object here is to provide you with extra materials you may use in any way you choose.

MORE ACTIVITIES - *Pygmalion*

1. Do a full production of *Pygmalion*.

2. Assign each student a character from the play. Each student should dress as that character, memorize a passage spoken by that character, and perform that passage in costume in front of the class.

3. Spend a class period discussing Greek legends, including Pygmalion. This could be a research project for students: each student could research one Greek legend. Have students give oral reports about their research.

4. Have students design a playbill for *Pygmalion*.

5. Have students design a bulletin board (ready to be put up, not just sketched) for *Pygmalion*.

6. Discuss your local dialect versus standard English. What colloquial phrases are there in your area?

7. Find a passage of written dialect and have students "translate" it into formal English.

8. Have students decide what about themselves they would like to improve, and have them devise a plan by which to achieve the improvement.

9. Spend a class period or so explaining the science of phonetics.

10. Have students do a movie review of the movie *My Fair Lady* after they see it.

11. Have students compare and contrast the movie of *My Fair Lady* with the book *Pygmalion*.

12. If your students have particularly casual speech, spend a class period or two doing some pronunciation drills with them.

WORD SEARCH - *Pygmalion*

All words in this list are associated with *Pygmalion*. The words are placed backwards, forward, diagonally, up and down. The included words are listed below the word searches.

```
Q P J E X V F Z N S D Y K F V L S H N J Z B N V
C H M R Y B Q P Z Y J F P Z R H Y C A K C G Z V
B R W J M N J J Y P Y D A L C E W H E Z Q F G N
F L O W E R S T A G E R A I N V D I G N I T Y C
F G Z D D H F F N L M M R N R U K D Y D E L W K
I J T S A R B I O S S A M S S K P Z Y D D W R Z
J M J W R S R R H R P C L T H M S G D T A W D N
P E A R C E S A C T D E B I D O O L I T T L E X
S T V G K N N A K Y C I E X O C P G I F B G D X
Y N W C I V C N B M N J M C D N T B Z P V B K Y
M H I G X N D M A M M B V Y H Q F M P G P Z V M
M P G C B W A B R M A R N E P O M M U C K E Y R
J I K M R A M T K L A P M N G R H X T K L G R D
H Y F T R N T T I G P N L X X T S D J R L D M S
G Z J A H R P B L O V X D G Q W M Z M V L V Q B
P W L G N S C U B D N Z R S G D C T X P D T P B
R C G L H G V S T J W B Q Y X G S Z W Z F L V R
```

ACT	FAIR	MANNERS	SCENE
AMBASSADOR	FLOWERS	NEPOMMUCK	SHAW
CLARA	FREDDY	PEARCE	SHOP
DIGNITY	HIGGINS	PICKERING	SLIPPERS
DOOLITTLE	IMAGINATION	PYGMALION	SPEECH
DUSTBIN	LADY	RAIN	STAGE
EYNSFORD	LIZA	RICH	VULGAR

CROSSWORD - *Pygmalion*

CROSSWORD CLUES - *Pygmalion*

ACROSS
1. To copy; to do exactly as another does
4. Having lots of money
6. Flower girl who becomes a lady
7. It is served in the afternoon with light cookies
10. The way one looks; appearance
11. Myself
13. Liza throws Higgins' ----- at him
15. Opposite of on
16. My ---- Lady; musical version of Pygmalion
17. Remember to say 'please' and '_____-you'
18. Eliza sold these
20. Play division
21. There are lots of rules about how to do this; ingest food
22. It goes with sugar at tea or coffee time
23. Rich people do this to their money; sum
24. 'She's deliciously low--so horribly dirty...Put her in the ---'
28. Adieu means --- we meet again
29. Liza gets her own flower ----
31. Politely take little drinks
33. Housekeeper for Higgins
34. Greasy substance; used as lubricant
36. Ingratiating manner
37. It's only ---. Low spirits and nothing else.
39. The final curtain falls at the ---
40. Definite article
41. Kind of language Eliza uses to tell the story of her aunt's death
43. Act division
44. No changes can be made unless you take the first ----
45. Aids

DOWN
2. Belonging to me
3. Tries to imitate Liza's manners
4. Gives the characters a believable motivation for meeting
5. The professor who transforms Liza
8. To have an effect
9. The colonel
12. More than is necessary
13. Author
14. He created a statue of a woman so beautiful he fell in love with her
16. Eliza marries him
19. Gentlewoman
20. He had a reception
21. ------ - Hill; mother and daughter
25. Higgins and Pickering both study this
26. Guest at ambassador's reception who was fluent in many languages
27. Eliza's last name
30. Social graces
32. Place where play is usually performed
35. Fashions
38. Book; fiction
42. Coordinating conjunction

CROSSWORD ANSWER KEY - *Pygmalion*

MATCHING QUIZ/WORKSHEET 1 - *Pygmalion*

___ 1. DOOLITTLE   A. Housekeeper for Higgins

___ 2. CLARA   B. Eliza marries him

___ 3. PYGMALION   C. Place where play is usually performed

___ 4. MANNERS   D. Gentlewoman

___ 5. SHOP   E. The colonel

___ 6. PICKERING   F. Author

___ 7. SHAW   G. Social graces

___ 8. HIGGINS   H. Tries to imitate Liza's manners

___ 9. SPEECH   I. Play division

___ 10. EYNSFORD   J. Kind of language Eliza uses to tell the story of her aunt's death

___ 11. FREDDY   K. ____ Hill; mother and daughter

___ 12. ACT   L. It's only ___. Low spirits and nothing else.

___ 13. IMAGINATION   M. He created a statue of a woman so beautiful he fell in love with her

___ 14. LADY   N. The professor who transforms Liza

___ 15. RICH   O. Having lots of money

___ 16. STAGE   P. Eliza's last name

___ 17. PEARCE   Q. Higgins and Pickering both study this

___ 18. SCENE   R. Liza gets her own flower ___

___ 19. FAIR   S. My ____ Lady; musical version of Pygmalion

___ 20. VULGAR   T. Act division

MATCHING QUIZ/WORKSHEET 2 - *Pygmalion*

___ 1. FLOWERS   A. He created a statue of a woman so beautiful he fell in love with her

___ 2. FREDDY   B. Eliza sold these

___ 3. LIZA   C. Eliza marries him

___ 4. FAIR   D. Liza throws Higgins' ____ at him

___ 5. DUSTBIN   E. Tries to imitate Liza's manners

___ 6. RAIN   F. Housekeeper for Higgins

___ 7. STAGE   G. It's only ____. Low spirits and nothing else.

___ 8. NEPOMMUCK   H. Guest at ambassador's reception who was fluent in many languages

___ 9. PICKERING   I. 'She deliciously low--so horribly dirty...Put her in the ____'

___ 10. VULGAR   J. The professor who transforms Liza

___ 11. PEARCE   K. Kind of language Eliza uses to tell the story of her aunt's death

___ 12. IMAGINATION   L. Play division

___ 13. ACT   M. Flower girl who becomes a lady

___ 14. CLARA   N. Author

___ 15. MANNERS   O. The colonel

___ 16. HIGGINS   P. Place where play is usually performed

___ 17. DOOLITTLE   Q. Eliza's last name

___ 18. SLIPPERS   R. My ____ Lady; musical version of Pygmalion

___ 19. PYGMALION   S. Gives the characters a believable motivation for meeting

___ 20. SHAW   T. Social graces

KEY: MATCHING QUIZ/WORKSHEETS - *Pygmalion*

Worksheet 1	Worksheet 2
1. P	1. B
2. H	2. C
3. M	3. M
4. G	4. R
5. R	5. I
6. E	6. S
7. F	7. P
8. N	8. H
9. Q	9. O
10. K	10. K
11. B	11. F
12. I	12. G
13. L	13. L
14. D	14. E
15. O	15. T
16. C	16. J
17. A	17. Q
18. T	18. D
19. S	19. A
20. J	20. N

JUGGLE LETTER REVIEW GAME CLUE SHEET - *Pygmalion*

SCRAMBLED	WORD	CLUE
RAOADAMBSS	AMBASSADOR	He had a reception
GASET	STAGE	Place where play is usually performed
OILDTETOL	DOOLITTLE	Eliza's last name
ANRI	RAIN	Gives the characters a believable motivation for meeting
ALYD	LADY	Gentlewoman
FDRYENOS	EYNSFORD	_____ Hill; mother and daughter
LPRSEPSI	SLIPPERS	Liza throws Higgins' _____ at him
ASRENMN	MANNERS	Social graces
UAVRGL	VULGAR	Kind of language Eliza uses to tell the story of her aunt's death
AARCL	CLARA	Tries to imitate Lisa's manners
HPSO	SHOP	Lisa gets her own flower _____
ISNHIGG	HIGGINS	The professor who transforms Liza
BDNSUTI	DUSTBIN	'She deliciously low---so horribly dirty...Put her in the _____'
CIGENPIRK	PICKERING	The colonel
MAGIIAINTNO	IMAGINATION	It's only ____. Low spirits and nothing else.
ICHR	RICH	Having lots of money
ENCES	SCENE	Act division
EECHSP	SPEECH	Higgins and Pickering both study this
TAC	ACT	Play division
EAEPRC	PEARCE	Housekeeper for Higgins
ERLOFSW	FLOWERS	Eliza sold these
ZAIL	LIZA	Flower girl who becomes a lady
WASH	SHAW	Author
RIAF	FAIR	My _____ lady; musical version of Pygmalion
GYIITDN	DIGNITY	Liza has this; sense of personal self worth
REDDYF	FREDDY	Eliza marries him
PUCMOEMKN	NEPOMMUCK	Guest at ambassador's reception who was fluent in many languages

VOCABULARY RESOURCE MATERIALS

VOCABULARY WORD SEARCH - *Pygmalion*

All words in this list are associated with *Pygmalion* with an emphasis on the vocabulary words chosen for study in the text. The words are placed backwards, forward, diagonally, up and down. The included words are listed below.

```
M K K F S X G B F V B B Q P S A L N X Y S V F J
Q Z C J I U C D I X M K Y C L E S A A P M Y R K
G X W B Q N O D T L T S C Q D I T U G E G L L H
C O N D E S C E N S I O N M A G N A N I M O U S
T I F P O B D O N P I O Z O E I N T I D D E T Y
R O T R U G R E R A E L U E I N M N H D E O D P
A G G N O R M O P R L R U S P T D P V H U R R V
R M H S A W G A U R I L E B H H P A E Q G P S P
K Z I S Y D Z A T G E G E M M V Y M C T J Y E F
G D M A H J E Y T I H C I C P A S R U I U S X R
B N M Q B X V P B O C A I B S T N K X G T O H F
W N Z T Y L H K J F R A M A L I O M Y C Z Y U J
D X H V T G E Y T H P Y L N T E M R O K F Z W S
R E M O N S T R A N C E T L R I Y M I S K D P Q
F M V P G D Q W T B R V K Y Y H N N X L J Q L W
P X X X Q C D D K Y V P C C D V B G Y Q Y T B F
C K P S R N C G F G L V N C W P C D L W T V Z P
```

AMIABLE	DOGMATICALLY	MISCELLANEOUS	REPUDIATES
ASUNDER	FROWZY	PEDANTIC	SOMNAMBULIST
BILIOUS	GUMPTION	PEREMPTORILY	TOGS
BROUGHAM	IMPETUOUS	PLINTH	ZEPHYR
CONDESCENSION	INCORRIGIBLE	PRODIGAL	DEMEAN
MAGNANIMOUS	PURGATORY	DEPRECIATING	MENDACITY
REMONSTRANCE			

VOCABULARY CROSSWORD - *Pygmalion*

VOCABULARY CROSSWORD CLUES - *Pygmalion*

ACROSS
1. Liza throws Higgins' ----- at him
4. Having lots of money
7. A block or slab on which a pedestal, column or statue is placed
10. Sloppy; slovenly
12. Something that is airy, insubstantial or passing
15. A place or condition of suffering, expiation or remorse
18. Unusual; different
19. Apart from each other in position or direction
20. Ingest food
21. Play division
22. Boldness or enterprise; initiative or aggressiveness
25. Short for professional
26. Gives the characters a believable motivation for meeting
27. Gentlewoman
28. A little sleep
29. Appearing as if experiencing gastric distress caused by a disorder of the liver
30. Mild-mannered
31. Liza has this; sense of personal self-worth
32. Move in rhythm with music
33. The professor who transforms Liza
35. My ---- Lady; musical version of Pygmalion
38. Opposite of down
40. By the book; following the rules exactly
42. Act division
43. The final curtain falls at the —
45. Restaurant tablecloths are often made of this fabric
47. Good wines are sealed with one
48. Eliza marries him
50. The colonel
51. Liza gets her own flower ----

DOWN
1. Author
2. Writing instrument
3. Exhale in weariness or relief
5. Flower girl who becomes a lady
6. Belittling
7. Rashly or wastefully extravagant
8. Clothes
9. Impulsive and passionate
11. Rejects the validity or authority of
13. Not allowing contradiction or refusal; commanding
14. Incapable of being corrected or reformed
16. An expression of protest, complaint or reproof
17. Friendly and agreeable
23. Begging
24. Money above the amount of the bill left for the waiter
31. To humble oneself
34. Higgins and Pickering both study this
36. Go faster than a walk
37. Social graces
39. Housekeeper for Higgins
41. Tries to imitate Liza's manners
44. Opposite of night
46. Saucer's mate
49. Mr. Doolittle to Eliza

VOCABULARY CROSSWORD - *Pygmalion*

VOCABULARY WORKSHEET 1 - *Pygmalion*

___ 1. An expression of protest, complaint or reproof
        a. Incorrigible
        b. Peremptorily
        c. Remonstrance
        d. Somnambulist

___ 2. Rejects the validity or authority of
        a. Amiable
        b. Mendacity
        c. Repudiates
        d. Togs

___ 3. Something that is airy, insubstantial or passing
        a. Zephyr
        b. Demean
        c. Asunder
        d. Repudiates

___ 4. A place or condition of suffering, expiation or remorse
        a. Purgatory
        b. Pedantic
        c. Brougham
        d. Impetuous

___ 5. A block or slab on which a pedestal, column or statue is placed
        a. Pedantic
        b. Condescension
        c. Plinth
        d. Gumption

___ 6. To descend to the level of one considered inferior
        a. Condescension
        b. Bilious
        c. Miscellaneous
        d. Preempt

___ 7. Incapable of being corrected or reformed
        a. Incorrigible
        b. Dogmatically
        c. Purgatory
        d. Brougham

Pygmalion Vocabulary Worksheet 1 Page 2

___ 8. Apart from each other in position or direction
       a. Brougham
       b. Asunder
       c. Peremptory
       d. Purgatory

___ 9. A closed four-wheeled carriage with an open driver's seat in front
       a. Zephyr
       b. Miscellaneous
       c. Gumption
       d. Brougham

___ 10. Courageously noble
       a. Peremptorily
       b. Incorrigible
       c. Magnanimous
       d. Zephyr

___ 11. Appearing as if experiencing gastric distress caused by a disorder of the liver
       a. Impetuous
       b. Brougham
       c. Bilious
       d. Pedantic

___ 12. Sleepwalker
       a. Bilious
       b. Brougham
       c. Magnanimous
       d. Somnambulist

___ 13. Begging
       a. Mendacity
       b. Prodigal
       c. Purgatory
       d. Magnanimous

___ 14. Having a variety of characteristics, abilities, or appearances
       a. Dogmatically
       b. Peremptorily
       c. Depreciating
       d. Miscellaneous

Pygmalion Vocabulary Worksheet 1 Page 3

___ 15. Friendly and agreeable
        a. Asunder
        b. Togs
        c. Amiable
        d. Impetuous

___ 16. Not allowing contradiction or refusal; commanding
        a. Condescension
        b. Repudiates
        c. Somnambulist
        d. Peremptorily

___ 17. Boldness or enterprise; initiative or aggressiveness
        a. Pedantic
        b. Zephyr
        c. Gumption
        d. Peremptorily

___ 18. Characterized by an authoritative, arrogant assertion of unproved or unprovable principles
        a. Dogmatically
        b. Frowzy
        c. Gumption
        d. Remonstrance

___ 19. To humble oneself
        a. Plinth
        b. Togs
        c. Zephyr
        d. Demean

___ 20. Impulsive and passionate
        a. Impetuous
        b. Repudiates
        c. Peremptorily
        d. Prodigal

VOCABULARY WORKSHEET 2 - *Pygmalion*

___ 1. ASUNDER		A. Belittling

___ 2. TOGS		B. Rashly or wastefully extravagant

___ 3. CONDESCENSION		C. Sleepwalker

___ 4. PLINTH		D. Something that is airy, insubstantial or passing

___ 5. INCORRIGIBLE		E. To descend to the level of one considered inferior

___ 6. DEPRECIATING		F. Boldness or enterprise; initiative or aggressiveness

___ 7. DEMEAN		G. Rejects the validity or authority of

___ 8. SOMNAMBULIST		H. A block or slab on which a pedestal, column or statue is placed

___ 9. MENDACITY		I. Appearing as if experiencing gastric distress caused by a disorder of the liver

___ 10. IMPETUOUS		J. Apart from each other in position or direction

___ 11. ZEPHYR		K. Begging

___ 12. BROUGHAM		L. To humble oneself

___ 13. MAGNANIMOUS		M. By the book; following the rules exactly

___ 14. BILIOUS		N. Clothes

___ 15. REPUDIATES		O. Friendly and agreeable

___ 16. GUMPTION		P. Courageously noble

___ 17. AMIABLE		Q. A closed four-wheeled carriage with an open driver's seat in front

___ 18. PEDANTIC		R. Impulsive and passionate

___ 19. PRODIGAL		S. A place or condition of suffering, expiation or remorse

___ 20. PURGATORY		T. Incapable of being corrected or reformed

KEY: VOCABULARY WORKSHEETS - *Pygmalion*

Worksheet 1	Worksheet 2
1. C	1. J
2. C	2. N
3. A	3. E
4. A	4. H
5. C	5. T
6. A	6. A
7. A	7. L
8. B	8. C
9. D	9. K
10. C	10. R
11. C	11. D
12. D	12. Q
13. A	13. P
14. D	14. I
15. C	15. G
16. D	16. F
17. C	17. O
18. A	18. M
19. D	19. B
20. A	20. S

VOCABULARY JUGGLE LETTER REVIEW GAME CLUES - *Pygmalion*

SCRAMBLED	WORD	CLUE
UGRYORPTA	PURGATORY	A place or condition of suffering, expiation or remorse
CATPIDEN	PEDANTIC	By the book; following the rules exactly
NCEMLUSLOSIAE	MISCELLANEOUS	Having a variety of characteristics, abilities, or appearances
DAYIENTCM	MENDACITY	Begging
OGPARILD	PRODIGAL	Rashly or wastefully extravagant
IOPMETEYPLRR	PEREMPTORILY	Not allowing contradiction or refusal; commanding
UTIMPONG	GUMPTION	Boldness or enterprise; initiative or aggressiveness
ADNEEM	DEMEAN	To humble oneself
DICOSNEOCNSNE	CONDESCENSION	To descend to the level of one considered inferior
ECAIRIPTNGDE	DEPRECIATING	Belittling
NTPHLI	PLINTH	A block or slab on which a pedestal, column or statue is placed
EDURSEIATP	REPUDIATES	Rejects the validity or authority of
AAYLIGLTDOCM	DOGMATICALLY	Characterized by an authoritative, arrogant assertion of unproved or unprovable principles
AMISLSUTBONM	SOMNAMBULIST	Sleepwalker
DEARNUS	ASUNDER	Apart from each other in position or direction
SUOTPIUEM	IMPETUOUS	Impulsive and passionate
WZFYRO	FROWZY	Sloppy; slovenly
HZEPRY	ZEPHYR	Something that is airy, insubstantial or passing
MAEBLIA	AMIABLE	Friendly and agreeable
OIIIEBLRRCGN	INCORRIGIBLE	Incapable of being corrected or reformed
IANSNMGAMOU	MAGNANIMOUS	Courageously noble
SUOLIBI	BILIOUS	Appearing as if experiencing gastric distress caused by a disorder of the liver
TMNRCNEORSAE	REMONSTRANCE	An expression of protest, complaint or reproof
OGST	TOGS	Clothes
MGUARBOH	BROUGHAM	A closed four-wheeled carriage with an open driver's seat in front

www.ingramcontent.com/pod-product-compliance
Lightning Source LLC
Chambersburg PA
CBHW051419070526
44584CB00023B/3489